A Healing Ministry

A Healing Ministry
My Recollections of Canon Jim Glennon

© 2007 Sid Eavis.

Eavis, Sidney, J., 1939- .
A Healing Ministry : My recollections of Canon Jim Glennon.

1st ed.
Bibliography.
ISBN 9780980333008 (pbk).

1. Glennon, Jim.
2. Anglican Church of Australia - New South Wales - Sydney.
3. Canons, Cathedral, collegiate, etc. - Australia - Biography.
4. Clergy - Australia - Biography.
I. Title.

283.94092

To purchase additional copies go to
www.canonjimglennon.com

Produced for the author by
Bookbound Publishing
PO Box 309, Ourimbah, NSW 2258
FreeCall 1800 628 058
www.bookbound.com.au

A Healing Ministry

MY RECOLLECTIONS OF CANON JIM GLENNON

SID EAVIS

In memory of my dear friend Canon Jim Glennon

Canon Jim Glennon — approx. 65 years of age

Biblical References

Acknowledgements

I would first acknowledge the influence of the Holy Spirit who brought inspiration and truth to this project; secondly, the role of my wife Jenny who was unwittingly the causative factor in bringing Jim Glennon and us together through her point of felt need — healing from cancer. Jenny's help in the early stages of the book's development, and her help with research, in Australia and in Ireland, has made the whole project possible.

Thanks are due to Fr Terence Dicks, and the healing ministry congregation of St. Mary's, Waverley, who encouraged me to embark upon this project and to persevere with it. In particular, I thank Robin Hutcheon of St. Mary's who undertook the "first read" of the manuscript and made a number of constructive comments.

Thanks to Zillah Williams who edited the book, to her husband Alan for helpful advice, and to Sally Chambers in Florida for added assistance.

I am indebted to Dorothy Bird for her research into the history of the property we now know as the Healing Ministry Centre Golden Grove Ltd.

Paul Glennon, Jim's cousin, made family photographs available and clarified many details about Jim's life. I deeply appreciate his help. It was Paul who encouraged Jim to go to Ireland in the early 80s in search of his roots, and it was as a result of this that Jenny and I followed in his footsteps and undertook further research in 2006.

Finally, I want to express my appreciation of the Dean and the Cathedral for continued support of the Healing Ministry in the iconic building in the very heart of Sydney.

Contents

Foreword

Healing as a ministry was central to Jesus Christ but, sadly, on the periphery of what the Church is about today. Jim Glennon's discovery of its significance is the concern of this book as it studies the remarkable life of a pioneer in the practice of healing. I got to know Jim when I paid an official visit to Sydney in the 90s. A larger than life individual walked into the vestry where I was robing, introduced himself as Jim and with all the naturalness that comes from Australians comfortable with their own skin, proceeded to address me as George! Jim, I think, saw me as a fellow Christian who also believed that God's power is still available for Christians today. He was fully aware that God used ordinary as well as special means of healing, and he was alert to remind everyone that God, known to us as Father through Jesus, is always at hand to empower, bless and heal. Sid Eavis' book also tells a story about a man who loved people and kept in touch with them. I was very moved when, having had a pasting at the hands of the English media, Jim wrote to me assuring me of his prayers and offering some healing words that strengthened me in my determination to carry on without faltering.

We sometimes hear the words "We shall not see his like again". That may well be true of Jim Glennon and, indeed, Jim would have been uncomfortable and horrified in his lifetime if there was any touch of glorifying his ministry. He wanted others to be like his Lord. But if this book helps others to rediscover the power of God's healing touch and to follow him more nearly, then I believe Him in Glory would be humbly delighted.

George Carey
Lord Carey of Clifton
Former Archbishop of Canterbury, 1991-2002

Introduction

My wife, Jenny, is alive today because of the Healing Ministry at St. Andrew's Cathedral in Sydney, Australia. This book is, in part, the story of her healing. That is, it is the story of the man God used to establish the Healing Ministry at the Cathedral.

I'm not a writer, which is not to say I can't read or write, but my professional background is that of an electrical engineer, designing and constructing power stations. Jenny and I were both born in the United Kingdom just prior to the Second World War, and our lives were dominated by the need to survive. A roof over our heads and regular food on the table, were not a part of our everyday experience. The house Jenny lived in was bombed and, due to incessant air raids, we were both evacuated out of areas of maximum risk—as were so many thousands of other families.

We grew up having an understanding of a kingdom, given that we were reigned over by King George VI, and, as subjects of his kingdom, our parents were deployed in its defence. Jenny's father was a submariner who died during the War, so she grew up fatherless, in addition to all the other troubles of that time. Just to give a flavour of life as it was then—we had no motor cars; and such things as TVs, vacuum cleaners, telephones and refrigerators were not a part of our household. Frozen peas had not yet been invented;

there were no such things as inflation or unemployment. Things didn't get better immediately after the war. Rationing of food and clothing continued for many years.

My father didn't offer me any advice about my future other than saying, after I had qualified, "Change jobs about every two to three years, and by the time you are 35 you will know what you want to do with your career." I so distinctly remember, on one occasion, handing in my notice of resignation from a generating authority. I would have been about 28 years "young" at the time. The Chief Engineer told me I was throwing my career away, since all I had to do was to wait until he retired in 25 years and I would have his job! Apart from anything else, my ambition was not tempered by patience, and the thought of waiting that long was unacceptable, so I moved on. My career path took me more into management, except that I maintained a "hands-on" approach to my work.

I mention these things because my professional niche, if I can use that expression, took me into an area of problem-solving, although I never considered difficulties as problems but as challenges. These challenges were to be addressed and solved using the academic qualifications and job skills I had developed in practice.

So, when Jenny was diagnosed with cancer in 1987, this was the mind-set I had when we consulted the medical profession. A problem to be solved. How wrong I was! At best the doctors were sympathetically unhelpful and, at worst, showed concern for the affected organ—not for us (least of all me) as human beings with any feelings. They would suggest that we try this, and then that, and if these didn't work, we could always try surgery—except that it wasn't guaranteed to be successful. It subsequently developed into "come and see me in six months" (if you are still alive)!

Jenny and I searched for answers. We looked at alternative lifestyles, alternative religions, alternative medicine. A myriad of alternatives were around like Yoga, Meditation, Tai Chi and many others.

Our search led us to a book by a Melbourne man, Dr Ian Gawler. His book, *You Can Conquer Cancer*, dealt with meditation and diet. Meditation to get the mind right, and diet to restore the immune system. We read his book and were inspired, to say the least. We were almost at the point of travelling to Melbourne to attend Dr Gawler's clinic, having met several people who had already been.

But our lives were to take a dramatic change of direction, because we first went to England on one of my combined business/holiday trips and visited my sister, Ruth, in Yorkshire.

Ruth gave Jenny Jim Glennon's books to read. Jenny sat up all night reading them and, the next day, my sister invited her to the local church where a deaconess would be paying her monthly visit to pray for people. Jenny knew nothing about deaconesses, since she was brought up a Catholic, but she knew she just had to go forward for prayer at that service. At the service the deaconess put her hands on her shoulders and asked her what blessing she would like to receive. Jenny was so distraught that she couldn't speak, but it didn't matter because, to her amazement, the deaconess knew all her needs. Jenny looked into her face, saw her smile, and wanted what she had — the Holy Spirit.

Two days later in a country church a lady prayed with Jenny and then said, "You're from Australia. When you get back, go and visit St. Andrew's Cathedral and my dear friend Canon Jim Glennon, a Spirit-filled man of God."

Jenny couldn't wait to get back to Australia to meet Jim. When we got home to Sydney she went to the Cathedral. As she stepped across the threshold, she was greeted by the Healing Ministry congregation and knew she had found her spiritual home.

All of a sudden we were human beings, with feelings and emotions — there was hope, there was a future. Indeed, Golden Grove (The Healing Ministry Centre Golden Grove Ltd) became a second home to both of us. We learned the importance of having a positive attitude towards healing and that it was so easy to fall into negativity. Jenny was healed — praise God, and before we really knew what had happened, we were leading the cancer ministry programme at Golden Grove and bringing others to their own faith position.

We enrolled at Moore College and studied theology for three years. This was at Jim's suggestion as he said we needed to gain understanding of the Scripture, of church history and Christian doctrine.

I knew Canon Jim Glennon for about twenty years and, having followed him around, taking notes and writing these up into website teachings, I came to know the man as well as his ministry. We shared in God's word, we shared in ministry, we shared in social interaction with overseas visitors and local dignitaries. We shared a friendship.

Jim learned about the healing ministry in the school of "hard knocks". There was never any support. He often told of a situation early in his ministry at the Cathedral, under Archbishop Gough. The Archbishop summoned him to his office to tell him he was to stop leading people up the garden path and giving them false hope in respect of healing. Jim's response was diplomatic. Instead of launching into an account of his own experience, he said, "Your Grace, may I ask your advice?" He was invited to continue, and said, "Can I ask Your Grace what does the New Testament say about healing?" He wasn't trying to be flippant—he was expecting a quote from James 5:14,15, on the basis of which there could have been some theological debate—but his question was met by complete silence. While Jim waited patiently it became painfully apparent that there was to be no answer and, as Jim later put it, "If I had waited for an answer I believe I would still be sitting there!"

When he suffered an emotional breakdown, due in part to overwork, there was nobody in the church, or in the medical profession, to whom Jim could turn for help. Like so many people with whom he would later cross paths in ministry, he turned to God when all else had failed. "Would that we could learn to depend upon God more", rings in my ears—an expression he used time and time again.

In many ways Anglican Church leaders still hold to this position, as do many members of the Church, particularly in the Diocese of Sydney where Evangelism is their declared priority even to the point of their being unable to help anyone with their immediate or "living" needs.

This might seem a strong statement but, to demonstrate the point, let me share with you a letter I sent to the Office of the Archbishop of Sydney when the then archbishop had invited Anglicans to share their views about declining numbers in church congregations. I discussed with Jim the idea of responding to this, and he said (as he usually did when someone came to him with an idea he considered worthy), "Very good, you go ahead and do it!"

I showed the letter to Jim before sending it and he found nothing disagreeable in its content, even saying it was constructive criticism.

Your Grace,

I am responding to your invitation … to present comment upon diminishing congregations in the Anglican Church.

As a practising Anglican Christian I perceive the Church does not meet people at their point of need, so they seek solace elsewhere. This may not be another church although it might be for a while, or it could include secular counselling or medical consultation. It's part of our human nature to search and we cannot blame them, after all we are created for fulfilment in love through fellowship in relationships with each other, as well as with God.

I believe the causative factor to be our focus upon the "Evangelical" such that this has directed clerics away from teaching the broader revelations in Scripture. I am not suggesting there is anything wrong with being "Evangelical" but as wonderful as Salvation is, it's only a part of the fullness of God's will for us. The restoration of The Kingdom is surely the fullness. The "Evangelical" focus does not equip us (or our clerics) to meet people at their point of need. Our teaching for the hereafter does not attract prospective Christians whose priorities are for the now. We need teaching on meekness, how to show compassion so as to meet every person at their level, lest we preach at them over their heads for eternal needs without trying to meet their earthly needs as well.

The side effects of this focus are the absence of teaching repentance and faith as well as how to deal with forgiveness and how to pray effectively "so that we do not doubt in our heart but believe."

As Christians surely we should react differently to the circumstances in which we find ourselves, and we can only do this if we receive a more broad teaching such as, what God has provided and how to draw upon His promises through repentance and faith. In this way we could embrace "Whatever you ask" as well as Salvation.

Thank you for inviting suggestions from laity, it is both refreshing and encouraging to be asked to contribute opinion.

In His love and service,

Signed …

With the letter I sent some hypothetical, but sadly very close to reality, examples:-

A Christian man went to his minister. "Reverend, I am having difficulty with my wife, we are not getting along and we don't even talk anymore, can you help me?" *"I am afraid this is outside my area of expertise but, here is the name of a marriage counsellor he is rather expensive so he must be good!"*

A Christian woman went to her minister. "Reverend, my teenage children are causing so much aggravation in our family I am at the stage of asking them to leave, can you help me?" *"There is a special school for teenagers with difficulties like hypertension disorders; perhaps they can help you."*

A young Christian lady went to her minister. "Reverend, I am suffering from extreme loss of energy, my doctor calls it chronic fatigue syndrome. I can't get a job and my Mum says if I don't stop lounging around the house she's going to kick me out. Can you help me?" *"Well, I can't do anything about your chronic fatigue syndrome but I can give you the address of a women's shelter where you can stay for a while."*

A Christian man went to his minister. "Reverend, my wife has cancer and is not well enough to look after the children, can you help me?" *"I am sure we can do something, I will arrange for some casseroles to be delivered so you have a meal and I shall get some of the ladies to roster some support for you (until your wife dies)."*

A young Christian man went to his minister. "Reverend, I have had this argument with my brother and it's affecting the whole family now. He told my girl friend bad things about me, which were not true and she dumped me. Now she's going out with him. My parents don't talk to me, neither does my brother nor my ex girl friend so I can't even tell them the truth. As soon as I try, they say they don't want to hear about it. Can you help me?" *"Well, I can't talk to any of them because they don't come to church and I don't think they would listen to me anyway. You are very young and I think the best thing you can do is to try and forget all about it. There are many more fish in the sea!"*

A young non-Christian person went to a minister. "Reverend, I am worried about what will happen to me when I die, can you help me?"

Question—of these six scenarios, which do you consider being the most likely to happen? Sadly the last rarely if ever happens but the other five happen all the time. Is the church equipped to handle the first five scenarios? Unfortunately not, but they are able to deal with the sixth since it is 'Evangelical'.

Even though these examples are hypothetical they are typical of the needs people have every day and they are also situations the Healing Ministry deal with every day.

Here is the reply from the Archbishop's Office:-

Thank you for what you have said. I would have to say though, that the greatest need of people is for salvation. When we do teach about the hereafter, it does give us a better perspective on the here and now. History has shown us that when Christians are concerned about people's eternal destiny, that they are more likely to also be involved in caring for the day to day needs.

Jim often quoted Jesus' words, "What I do you will do too." He didn't only mean that he could do it too—he meant that we could do it too—all of us. We need to obey and trust, but he would say that we don't obey any more than we trust, because we think we have to understand everything first, so our intellect gets in the way of God's blessings.

Notwithstanding certain controversy surrounding the Healing Ministry, Jim never discarded Anglican doctrine, and held to the 39 Articles of Religion for the Anglican Church. He was, in fact, more true to the (complete) Bible than many who challenged his position regarding healing. There were few, if any, who actually challenged him to his face. Perhaps they knew better than to question something they quite clearly didn't understand!

Jim was often asked, "What is the Healing Ministry?" by which was really meant, "How does it work in order to draw upon this blessing?" Quite reasonably, people wanted to know what to do to be healed. This was his reply, "The Healing Ministry is knowing what God has provided, and acting upon it through repentance and faith." He would often add, "Simple it is; easy it is not!"

My purpose in writing this book is to keep Canon Jim Glennon's teachings alive, because, as he would have said, "Faith is not in fact for salvation alone any more than it is for healing alone. The Bible says it is for "whatever you ask for in prayer" (Mark 11:24).

I have opened each chapter with one of Jim's typical sayings. I call them "Glennonisms" — something, however, Jim did not feel comfortable about. I think this was because, in everything he did, he always wanted to give God the glory, and a "Glennonism" suggested, to Jim at least, that it might glorify him personally. I don't think we need to be quite as sensitive. I like to remember these sayings as being representative of his teaching. Accordingly, I view them simply as sayings which express spiritual truths in everyday language. I'm not suggesting he necessarily composed them himself, and apologise for not knowing who the authors might be. Some of them are his own, but in any event, all of us who heard him will identify with their depth of spiritual meaning.

I have closed each chapter with "An Anecdote" and need to make the point that neither of these opening or closing items necessarily have anything to do with the subject matter of the particular chapter. My hope is that they will trigger fond memories of Jim for you as they do for me, as well as shed light on the person and ministry of my friend, Canon Jim Glennon.

As mentioned elsewhere, the material in this book, unless otherwise stated is drawn from my own recollection of Jim's spoken teaching. I have added, in Part Two, written notes, which as Executor of Jim's Estate, I located in his personal papers. These include his experiences of being a Charismatic in a non-Charismatic Church as well as a series of three Sermon Notes presented at St. Andrew's

Cathedral, under the broad heading, "Three Main Themes of the Healing Ministry". Furthermore, and for the reader's enjoyment and edification, I have included a CD of Jim preaching in his unique style, the subject being what he called, "An Overview of the Healing Ministry", recorded at St. Mary's Church, Waverley, on December 16, 2004. To share another Glennonism, I believe everyone who listens to this will be blessed "out of their socks!"

Sid Eavis

Part One

1

The Irish connection

A GLENNONISM

Stop saying how sick you are by sight;
start saying how well you are by faith!

In March 2006 Jenny and I were in England visiting relatives, and the opportunity to cross over to Ireland, where the Glennon family had its roots, was too good to miss.

Following Jim's death in 2005 I had organised his funeral and, as executor of his will, had sorted out his personal affairs. I had begun writing my reminiscences of him and his teaching, and wanted to see if we could learn more about his Irish ancestors.

In Ireland we experienced a richness of ancestral awareness in everyone we met, together with a willingness to share their history without resentment towards the English Parliament, or even perhaps towards us as having English origins. Consequently, there was much more to learn than we had ever expected.

There were two major elements supporting the existence of what might be called the non-aristocratic community in Ireland some 150 years ago, one being "peat" which was freely available to those who had the strength to dig it out of the ground, providing fuel for cooking and warmth in the hovels in which they lived. The other was the humble "potato", the staple diet of this basic community. It was the latter that surely influenced the Glennon family to seek a new life in Australia all those years ago. I am referring to the mid 1800s when Jim's grandparents left Ireland soon after the potato blight struck in 1845. Before the potato blight, Ireland's population was about eight million. Millions died of starvation, mostly in the first year. The Irish population today is only about four million!

We thought to start by visiting Jim's maternal great-great-great grandmother's home "Kiltanon", knowing only that Jim's house in Clovelly, New South Wales, was called "Kiltanon" and it was also his father's and his uncle's middle name. Jim's ancestor on his mother's side was an O'Halloran who had married a Maloney. They lived on an estate called "Kiltanon" in County Clare in the southwestern farmlands of Ireland. The names O'Halloran, Maloney and Glennon are anglicised versions of the original Gaelic names but it was not too difficult to track down the origins of these families.

The directions we had were to drive southwest from Dublin to Limerick and then head north towards Galway passing, en route, a village called Tulla. Continuing further north about four kilometres towards Gort we were supposed to find the ruins of Kiltanon House but all we could find was a signpost "To Kiltanon House". Since this was by way of being a pilgrimage for us, Jenny took my photograph at this milestone in our journey. After much driving around the country lanes we were unable to locate any further directions, or indeed the ruined house. Having travelled such a distance from Australia we were not going to leave without some explanation, so we knocked on doors—any doors!

One of the amazing things about Ireland is the extent to which almost everyone we encountered was an amateur historian. They were able to provide quite personal information about the reasons behind certain events which took place in Ireland involving their particular relatives. There is a lively awareness of past events which have shaped the present, unlike my own experience where, after only a couple of generations, family history has faded from memory. The Irish have this inbuilt desire to hold on to this important family information.

Ireland was a staunch Roman Catholic enclave even before the arrival of Oliver Cromwell in 1649. King Charles I had been beheaded that same year, and Cromwell took control as Lord Lieutenant and General for the Parliament of England. A fanatical Protestant, Cromwell ruled with an iron rod, offering no mercy to those he called the "papist rebels" who had massacred English and Scottish settlers. He simply confiscated land from Irish owners to pay off his troops and those who had financed his parliamentary ambitions. The Protestant aristocracy, who often acted as absentee landlords, were on many occasions just as ruthless as Cromwell in denying any reasonable standard of living for the working man.

One would have expected to find an undercurrent of resentment between Catholics and Protestants, yet the issue of religious differences as written up in history books didn't match our experience of the people of either denomination. During, and after the time of Cromwell, inter-marriage was quite normal, and family ties created through marriage cemented stronger loyalties than religious differences. Some families even decided to adopt Protestantism in order to protect at least half the family assets (mainly productive land and the farm) and a lifestyle that would otherwise be denied because of their Catholicism. Such decisions were not so much motivated through greed or even good financial management but through the absolute need for survival.

One door-knock led us to a lady who invited us in, and who produced Ordnance Survey maps of the area to show us the extent of the Kiltanon Estate, which was originally 10,500 acres. She suggested that, before we actually visited the ruin, we should go and see a certain local amateur historian, Patrick O'Halloran who, we were to find out, was a relative of Jim's great-great-great grandmother O'Halloran. This most helpful lady described how to find the house where Patrick lived. She said we should go back to Tulla, and described an intersection beside which was a house that looked derelict. We found it. It didn't just look derelict—it was literally falling down. Having located his home, we introduced ourselves and took photos of Patrick while he answered questions about the Glennons.

We took a couple of photos of his house and, where it looks as if the roof has fallen in—it has! As we walked into the back yard, the front door being nailed up, we could see his water supply stored in old wooden barrels and pots in the back yard. No running water, no heating other than a peat fire on which he cooked. There was a big black iron pot hanging over the fire, simmering away. I dread to think what he was cooking, or maybe he was washing his socks. As one looked up to the ceiling it was pitch black from years and years of smoke, the entire building sighed in advancing years as did Patrick.

It was good to talk to Patrick O'Halloran before visiting the Estate, since it was as if he was still living in that era. It certainly gave us a flavour of life in Ireland, hitherto unknown to us. He is 83 years old and looks a tad older due to having been the victim of a house invasion which included a very serious bashing. However, there was nothing wrong with his long-term memory. He shared the following story with us; one might consider it to be folklore but it has a ring of "Irish truth" about it. The story has to do with a chance meeting between two men travelling on horseback along a (then) track between Limerick and Galway. One of the men was a Cromwellian soldier who was absolutely fed up with the cold weather since it was snowing and blowing a fierce easterly wind. Both men had sought shelter in a church and, after some discussion, the Cromwellian soldier asked if the other gentleman knew anyone who would give him his fare for the passage back home to England. After a while the Cromwellian produced the title deed of a property and offered it for sale if the gentleman could come up with some money. The gentleman emptied his pockets and, although it was only a few shillings, a deal was struck. The story has it that the title deed was for the estate known as "Kiltanon", and that the gentleman's name was Maloney!

James Maloney of Ballinahinch and Kiltanon was a Justice of the Peace and served in O'Brien's Regiment of Foot in support of King James II. His property was saved by the Treaty of Limerick through a clause which exempted those within the city's walls from having their property confiscated. In 1702 he built the family vault at St. Mochulla's graveyard. His uncle, John Maloney, born in 1619 was Canon of Rouen and Bishop of Killaloe from 1672 to 1689.

I think Jim would have loved to have known he was not only descended from men of the cloth but that he had Protestant origins, including a Bishop, going back to the sixth century.

Patrick told us that his father was 20 years old in 1923 when Kiltanon House was destroyed by fire, and that he knew who did it, and why. His father had worked for the Maloneys on the Kiltanon Estate and said that the head gardener was a Scot called Stuart. For reasons unknown to Patrick, Col. Maloney had dismissed him. A short time later, when the Maloneys were away on a trip, Stuart set fire to the house as retribution, and watched it burn. The house is located miles away from anywhere, and in any event, there were no fire brigades or even running water to help put out the fire, even if there was anyone around to do it. It was razed to the ground, with the exception of one corner.

Patrick told us where to locate the ruin and said that, as we approached the Estate, we would find a grand entrance with beautiful 19th century wrought-iron gates hung on sandstone columns. From the Ordnance Survey maps we could see the outline of the house and outbuildings within the lanes and stone walls that surrounded the property. We had virtually driven around the perimeter of the Estate.

As we searched for the actual site of Kiltanon House, we happened across a farm gate and a track. A farmer on a tractor was coming along, and was surprised to see anyone out there in the sticks. There was a sign on the gate "No Entry Keep Out" but we climbed over and told the farmer who we were, and why we had come. We asked if he could show us where the house had been, and he pointed over the gate to the site of the building. He leased some of the land from the present owner and told us about the property, which had recently been sold. The people who had owned it, and lived there for the previous five years or so, were called Stuart—funny that! They had sold it to a businessman who was an antique furniture dealer who was in the process of building a warehouse on the site of the original house. The building as we saw it was a steel girder frame, in-filled with brick, and with a steel roof. Far from finished, the end wall was open and there was no floor. The wrought-iron gates were lying in the long grass, and the sandstone columns had been demolished to facilitate access for building machinery. The replacement gate was a galvanised tubular steel frame, and we were pleased Jim had not seen this degradation.

As we stood on the grass verge in front of the warehouse, the

7

farmer told us that there were underground rooms, accessed by secret tunnels from the original house. These were to provide a hiding place for the family in the event of an attack.

Kiltanon in Gaelic is written Coillte ainin, which means woods of fire. It is listed in a book of historic buildings as being a ruin and uninhabitable. The original building in which the Maloneys lived was an early 19th century (1833) brick, three-storey, hip-roofed house with a stone-facing, overlooking extensive parkland to the south. The view is still there! There was a two-storey return and a one-storey wing attached to the west side of the house. The main drive was approached from the southeast and crossed over the Toomeens River near where it disappears underground. There was a courtyard to the north of the house and a farmyard some distance to the west. There was also another farmyard to the southwest.

When Jim had visited this Estate in the late 1980s he had "liberated" one of the remaining bricks from the ruin by prising it out with the wheel brace from his hire car. He brought it back to Australia as a memento and had it cut into three, a third for himself, and a third each for his brother Stephen and cousin Paul.

Jim shared a sad family experience with me some time after his trip to Ireland. He told me that his father had not attended his ordination! This was because his father was Catholic, albeit lapsed, and he couldn't, or wouldn't, understand why his son would want to be a minister in the Anglican Church.

While in Ireland, Jim tried to trace his family history by looking in Catholic Church records. He drew a blank, and said it was as if the Glennons simply didn't exist in Ireland. Then, someone suggested he try looking in the Anglican Church records, and there he found them! His grandparents were married in Limerick in the Anglican Church. This news dissolved Jim's feelings of resentment towards his father who had suggested he had taken the wrong doctrinal direction. He said afterwards, "I am so glad I have found out I had Anglican roots. I was meant to be an Anglican after all."

Now Jim knew that his grandparents were Anglican. However, a mystery still existed regarding his father having Catholic roots. His grandparents sailed from England to Australia on the Mermaid in 1855 as Anglicans, and disembarked in Melbourne as Catholics.

We can only presume that there was a very active Catholic chaplain on board the Mermaid! This mystery will live on since we have no way of getting to the truth.

As you read on, you will see that, for many years, Jim faced several trials of various kinds which tested his faith. He was not well received in ecclesiastical circles because of his different approach to the Scriptures and, in particular, his declared belief that God's healing is available today. This situation did of course change as he gained respect within the church, but to start with he was nothing short of an outcast. His focus was so strong that even though his father's attitude, as well as that of his peers and superiors in his own church, brought him much sorrow and anguish, he persevered in his belief. I would like to think that Jim had inherited his determination to "never give up" from his Irish forbears. One of his favourite Bible quotations is revealing of this character trait:

Consider it pure joy my brothers, whenever you face trials of many kinds because you know that the testing of your faith develops perseverance. Perseverance must finish its work so that you may be mature, and complete, not lacking anything. (James 1:1-4)

AN ANECDOTE

When Jenny and I first knew Canon Jim, we became involved in some social interaction and invited him out for lunch. We took him to our favourite fine dining restaurant where there was an extensive á la carte menu. Gentleman that he was, Jim would not order until my wife Jenny had ordered, and she indulged in ordering some exotic dishes. Jim looked up from the menu, made direct eye contact with the waiter and said, "Do you do fish and chips?" Jenny and I were mortified! The waiter graciously responded, "We can do anything, sir", so fish and chips he had.

Some years later Jim, Jenny and I were entertaining guests from the USA, and were dining at Doyle's, Watson's Bay. For those who don't know, this is a well-known seafood restaurant, so everything on the menu was fish of some description. As we enjoyed a pre-dinner drink, Jim waved at a lady at another table and she came over to say hello. Jim introduced her. It was Mrs Doyle. After some small talk she returned to her table and Jim turned to me saying, "She proposed marriage to me some time ago." "How so?" I asked, given that she was already married. "Oh it was just a joke", said Jim, "but we can all dream." I was wondering what he would dream about, when he added, "Just think of it, Sid. I could have fish and chips every day."

On another occasion we were invited out, with others, to one of Jim's birthday lunches. We didn't know if an ordained minister drank in public—alcohol, that is. The drinks waiter started to take orders and went round the table of about 12 guests. The first person ordered a tomato juice, and the next a lemonade. We followed suit, and Jim was the last to order. "I'll have a gin and tonic," he said, and we all felt short-changed! So clergymen do like a drink, we thought. Jim's birthday was early December, and as Christmas followed soon after, the word was out that gave everyone the same idea for Jim's Christmas present. We saw him shortly after Christmas and he told us he had enough gin to take a bath in the stuff!

Above
Sid Eavis and Patrick O'Halloran discussing Kiltanon House, 2006

Right
Patrick O'Halloran in his house at Tulla, Ireland, 2006

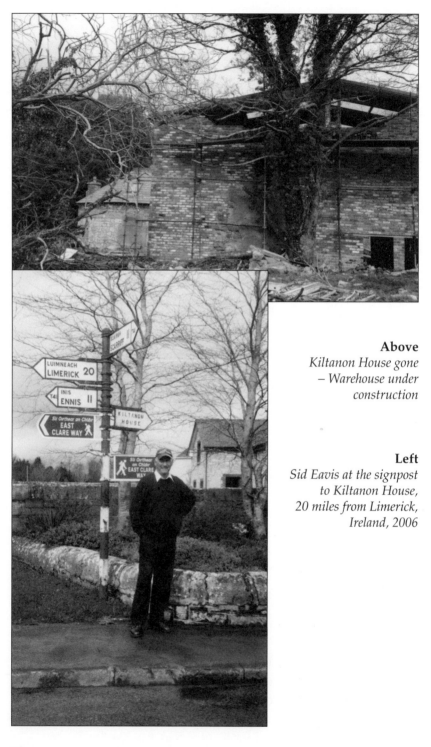

Above
*Kiltanon House gone
– Warehouse under
construction*

Left
*Sid Eavis at the signpost
to Kiltanon House,
20 miles from Limerick,
Ireland, 2006*

2

In the beginning

We know little of Jim's childhood years. He was born into a middle class family on the 2nd December 1920 at Double Bay, New South Wales. The family lived at Clovelly, a coastal suburb of Sydney, Australia.

His father, John Kiltanon Glennon, had met his mother, Marguerite (Madge) Bessie Florence (née Traynor), in South Africa during the Boer War through a connection between their respective parents.

Jim was a student at Randwick High School before joining the Army in August 1942. It was during army training that he suffered the loss of his left eye, owing to an artillery accident. This meant that he wasn't sent to serve overseas. His rank, on discharge in October 1946, was that of Staff Sergeant.

It was during this time that Jim studied for the Matriculation

Examination, which he passed in 1945. After leaving the Army he enrolled at Moore Theological College.

He had been converted in his teen years at a mission conducted by the late Canon Arrowsmith, but didn't go to Moore College with a passion for service for the Lord or even with the intention of being ordained. It wasn't until after three curateships that he developed what he thought was his mission in the Church—administration. This was what he was good at. For example, he single-handedly, organised a visit to the Cathedral by Queen Elizabeth and Prince Phillip. It was not really until after 1960 when he started the healing ministry that this direction changed.

His father was an electrician. His mother stayed at home, caring for the family, as the custom was in those days. Jim was the first-born and had two brothers, Keith Leslie Glennon and Stephen John Glennon. Notwithstanding a congenital condition that affected all the brothers, Jim outlived them both by several years.

Because Jim's father was not a practising Catholic, and his mother didn't become a Christian until much later in life, there was neither a spiritual upbringing, nor any example of Christian values in the Glennon household during Jim's formative years.

Memories of his childhood were coloured by feelings of insecurity and fear; he told, for example, of hiding behind a chair if someone even knocked on the front door. This insecurity grew in his teen years, and further increased as he became an adult. The effect of this was that he shied away from any relationships, even casual friendships. He felt threatened by all but his immediate family, and coped with life by building emotional walls around himself as a means of protection. He was able to convince himself that his only bad memories were from his childhood. He had acquaintances, but always kept a healthy distance so as not to become involved in anything that would confront his insecurity. Fear was always present and he didn't just fear making an acquaintance, but was afraid of the fear that accompanied his every thought.

He took up two curacies in Sydney, first at St. Oswald's Haberfield and later at St. John's Darlinghurst. He then took up the position of curate at St. Martin in the Bull Ring, Diocese of Birmingham, UK, where Canon Bryan Green was the rector. This was where he received his main pastoral training. After this, he was for a short time at St. Augustine's College, Canterbury, the Central College of the Anglican Communion.

On his return to Sydney, and at the instigation of Archbishop Mowll, he studied Social Science at Sydney University, specialising in casework and the psycho-social development of children. He hadn't wanted to do the Social Science course, but was subsequently grateful because it equipped him for ministry. He was given some advice at the time by Canon Marcus Loane—later to become Archbishop Loane—who told him, "God does not show us the end at the beginning. He gives us enough light for one step at a time."

Also at this time he was appointed to the staff of St. Andrew's Cathedral where he took on a variety of duties. Concurrently, and for a period of seven years, he taught Pastoral Method at Moore Theological College and supervised senior theological students in clinical pastoral education in Sydney Hospitals.

Jim's brother Stephen married, but very late in life and had no children, while Jim and his other brother Keith were life-long bachelors. It was his brother Stephen and their cousin Paul Glennon who first became interested in the family's history. It was their research which established the fact that the family had sailed from Liverpool in England on the Mermaid in 1855 bound for Melbourne, and that prior to this time they had, for ten years, lived in Manchester. And it was at their suggestion that Jim did some research of his own when he went overseas for a preaching engagement.

Jim Glennon had what might be called his "Old Testament" period when he was aware of God, yet there was a distance between them—not quite a separation but certainly a distance. As has already been mentioned, he spent the first 40 years of his life living in fear and insecurity, so he was certainly in the wilderness but, praise God, he came to know the risen Christ, and the next 45 years of his life were on the Kingdom plane—his "New Testament" period. His awareness of God grew as he journeyed through life, drawing upon the Word of God for salvation as well as for healing and wholeness—in fact for, "whatever you ask for" (Mark 11:24). In this respect he stood in faith for many, ultimately bringing them to their own faith position. "Faith", Jim would say, "was not for healing alone, not for salvation alone, it was for 'whatever'."

Jim would often talk about the "big picture" as revealed to us in the Bible, and would draw attention to the words of Jesus recorded in Mark's gospel:

Jesus went into Galilee proclaiming the good news of God, 'The time has come,' he said. 'The Kingdom of God is near. Repent and believe the good news!' (Mark 1:14-15).

The gospel means "good news" and is all about the Kingdom, not salvation. Jim would often say, "Salvation (as wonderful as it is) is but a means to an end." Saving souls was, however, just as important to him as meeting people's particular needs for healing and wholeness.

From time to time Jim heard God speak to him directly. One such occasion was just after his ordination. Colleagues were offering themselves for service in the mission field, and a young Jim did the same. But, instead of God sending him off to Africa or the like, He said to him, "You are to learn how to pray." Obediently, Jim searched the Scriptures to gain understanding about prayer, and he not only learned how to pray, but made prayer the cornerstone of his teaching ministry. He lived his life by faith and not by sight, and was absolute in his belief that the promises of God are available today for all believers, through repentance and faith. However, before he reached that point in his life he had to work through a major trial, one which was to shape the whole of the rest of his life and ministry.

AN ANECDOTE

I learned of the following experience only very recently at a church function when people were reminiscing about their childhood. Jim was a youth leader early in his ministry and had taken a group of youngsters away on a camp. The person who shared this story was one of the youngsters. They were all sleeping in a dormitory-type shack and, as young kids do, they wanted to "muck-up", but every time they looked over towards Jim he was (apparently) still awake, watching them with one eye open.

The kids didn't know about Jim's accident, and that he wore a glass eye which didn't close. They believed he was watching them all night, and eventually gave up waiting, and fell asleep!

Left
*Jim (seated) age 9 years
with his two younger
brothers Keith and
Stephen*

Right
*Jim's grandmother Laura
Elizabeth nee-Traynor
with baby Jim*

18

Above
*The Glennon family with
Jim's grandmother Laura*

Left
*Jim's grandmother Laura,
Jim and brother Keith*

3

Breakdown

A GLENNONISM

When we exercise faith in God—what we believe—
we have to hold to it so it becomes a way of life,
without so much as putting in a comma or a full stop!

Jim was 40 when he had his nervous breakdown, marking the end of his "Old Testament" period. An avalanche of past emotions engulfed him. He described his life at that time as being like a negative film being developed—slowly coming into focus from his thoughts, his fears—before his very eyes. He just could not stop it happening as he stood frozen in front of this developing image of himself and his circumstances. He further described this dark period of his life as being full of torment; he had not yet become aware of the Bible verse which says, *"What I feared has come upon me; what I dreaded has happened to me."* (Job 3:25).

Reflecting on this terrible situation, Jim told me that there were times, too many times, when death would have been a blessed release. There seemed no answer to his predicament; the doctor couldn't help, nor could the psychiatrist or social worker. There was sympathy, even empathy, but no compassion. It never occurred to him that the church should have been able to help him at his desperate point of felt need. This was not surprising, since his theological training in the Sydney Diocese was evangelical, and his need at this point was not salvation but healing. He had a "living" problem not a "dying" problem.

Long before this Jim had thought that Christianity, in no small measure, lacked the capacity to meet people at their various everyday points of need. Not much has changed in 40 years, except that mainstream church congregations have diminished and continue to diminish. Dealing with such situations as loneliness, grief, emotional stress, rejection and resentment, quite apart from physical "dis-ease", is not generally on the church agenda. In those early days, Jim's understanding of the words of James 5:13–15 was that they were just words:

> *"Is any one of you in trouble? He should pray. Is anyone happy? Let him sing songs of praise. Is any one of you sick? He should call the elders of the church to pray over him and anoint him with oil in the name of the Lord. And the prayer offered in faith will make the sick person well; the Lord will raise him up. If he has sinned, he will be forgiven."*

When, later, he became aware of its meaning and context, this passage was to become the blueprint of his ministry.

Depression, insecurity, fear—call it what you will—these emotions were not peculiar to clergymen, engineers, or even psychiatrists. They affected the entire population in various forms, and Jim was later to draw comfort from the Scripture, *"For God hath not given us the spirit of fear; but of power, and of love, and of a sound mind."* (2 Timothy 1:7 KJV).

There was a clue for him from an experience he had shortly after his conversion, but he was unable to see it at the time. At the Mission service, held in his parish church in Clovelly, when Jim had raised his hand as an outward sign that he was accepting Christ and "making a decision", the missioner, Canon Arrowsmith, asked, "Are you sure you have accepted Christ?" Jim replied, "Yes". But nothing changed after the mission as far as he was aware. Weeks went by, then he went to his rector, the late Howard Dillon, and told him that nothing had changed. His rector said, "You will never be converted like that." Jim asked what he was doing wrong. Rev. Dillon introduced him to Hebrews 11:1, *"Now faith is the substance of things hoped for, the evidence of things not seen."* (KJV). Referring to Mark 11:23,24, he told Jim that faith is believing it before you see it. You have to believe you have received these things so that you do not doubt in your heart. He went on to say that you don't do these things with your feelings; you do it with your mind.

John Stott, the famous theologian, and author of several books said, "Your mind matters." Well, still nothing happened, but now Jim was no longer saying, "But it's not working." Now he was disciplining his mind to say, "I have accepted Christ, I have made a decision. I have been saved, and I believe it before I see it." He said it was nearly two years before he had a witness of the Spirit that God was in his life.

The next significant event in Jim's life was not planned, at least not by him. He was working at the Cathedral, and for some reason had gone out for a walk. He said he thought it was because of a disagreement with a particular staff member. He was unable to recall the details, but suffice it to say he remembered that his emotion at the time was one of fear. As he walked around the corner into George Street he passed a cinema and, not knowing why—because he was not much of a cinema-goer, nor was he attracted by the title of the particular movie being shown—he went in and watched the film. When he came out a couple of hours later he realised that, during the time spent watching the film, he had not been afraid; he was totally emotionally engaged with the film. As his usual emotions flooded back into his mind he felt the fear overwhelming him again, since he now had to return to the Cathedral and the person he had failed to confront. It was at times like this that he despaired, because the other person never appeared to be emotionally affected, and yet he himself seemed to be forever emotionally trapped in these situations.

He asked himself why fear was absent from his mind during that brief escape into the cinema. He subsequently addressed that question, drawing upon what he called the "back burner of his mind", until he came up with the solution—that it was because his mind was exclusively occupied with something else! He was confident he had found the key to his problem, and decided he would develop this dynamic.

He was still in his wilderness, feeling separated from God, and if there were angels in attendance he didn't feel their presence. His abject misery dominated his every thought and action. The solution to his problem was to come from his recognition that it all started with the mind.

The following is his own description of his experience:-

When there is a real breakdown of ego-functioning you become a different person to what you have been all your life up to that point. There is something of the Jekyll and Hyde about it. The new you is different and unpredictable. You have new motivations but lack of old restraints. On the surface you try to appear normal but underneath you are a pack of ravening wolves. Fear grips you because you can't always control them. They break out and you are different. Friends and acquaintances are mystified. You would like to explain, but what can you say? If you don't understand something yourself it's no good trying to unravel it for someone else. That is where you ask question after question; but there are no answers. For me it was a "dark night of the soul".

I could blame other people for the circumstances that brought about my trouble, and this I did, not a little. The devil of resentment is that it is justified—at least, we believe it is. There is a natural tendency to "pass the buck" and leave someone else to hold it.

When everything was as bad as it could be, when there was nothing left to draw on and nowhere else to turn, something happened that changed my life. God spoke to me again. "Is there anything you can learn out of all this?" The words were formed in my mind in an indelible way. I can remember them as though they were yesterday. Nothing like it had happened before. Some people affirm that they have a kind of "hot line" with God; I am not one of them. But, on this occasion, I knew the reality of hearing the voice of God. Since then, and over twenty-five years, there have been four other times when the same kind of thing happened, and all of them have been times of extreme need. As far as my experience goes it is when we are at the end of our tether that God is able to be strong in what He says and does.

As I have said, it was the one question that had not been asked. It had never occurred to me that there was something to learn from all my difficulties. I could but listen. But there was more, because God went straight on to say, "You are to learn to depend on me more". When the Holy Spirit speaks, you not only know what He says, you also know what He means. Both the message and the meaning were crystal clear to me.

Before this, when I prayed about my problems it was with the idea of God helping me with them — "If it be thy will". Whatever else this did, it did nothing for my problems; they only got worse until I couldn't carry on. Something else said in church circles to those in need is, "God's grace is sufficient for you".[1] I didn"t minimise that, but the way it is used seems a substitute for doing something that would make a difference to the burden being carried. Frankly, I don't think the church knows much about drawing on God's help so that the circumstances of life are changed in a tangible way. It does no more than employ a community resource with "Amen" on the end and has a theology that is a "let-out".

But now, despite the breakdown and all that it meant, things were suddenly and wonderfully different. In a moment of revelation a whole new understanding had been given as to how I was to react to my circumstances. Despair became hope, fear became faith and my arm was strengthened for whatever lay ahead.

The problems were still there but they were no longer "rubbing me out". Now they were doing something for me: they were to become the reality with which I was to depend upon God more. It was a kind of transposition — one thing became another. Instead of the previous idea of God helping me with my difficulties, now my difficulties were

---

1   2 Corinthians 12:9

helping me with God. It was a turn around. Before, God was (as it were) behind me and I was looking at the mountain. Now, there had been an about-turn so that it was the mountain that was behind me and I was looking at God. This meant that, instead of homing in on my problems, my problems were to enable me to home in on God. This is what I was to learn; this is what I had to do.

When you are in the middle of a wood you don't come out straight away even when you have at last got on the right path. And I was in the middle of my wood. Every day I had to discipline my prayer-thinking so that the permitted difficulties in my life were changed into the reality with which I turned to God, moved towards Him and depended on Him in mind and heart. It was a tremendous relief to at least know what to do, and I persevered with it until it came out right.

I continued in prayer until I was inwardly and meaningfully depending on God alone. When that position was reached I experienced a deep, quiet oneness with God that was all-pervading. If, after resting in the Spirit, a problem slipped around the corner so that it began to worry me again, I would put it behind me and come back to affirming my oneness with God. In the best sense of the word, it was putting the positive in place of the negative. The next day I went through the same procedure again.

It was never easy and I frequently got it wrong. One of the things I learnt was that it was vital to begin the day right. It was no good starting off with a worry session or a hate session and then trying to come to joy and peace in believing later on. Neither could one wait for one's more formal time of prayer before beginning to pray. The pressure of my old anxieties was still heavy upon me so I had to affirm my dependence on God before I was even out of bed and continue it while brushing my teeth, driving my car and, in a corner of my mind, whatever else I was doing later on. Not infrequently it meant holding on for dear life so that this was being done every moment of the day. It was no virtue on my part; I got it right because there was no alternative; it was a self-survival exercise.

It might help if some more detail is given as to how I went about doing this. It was one thing to know what to do and another to know how to do it. Well, I learnt by trial and error. The really important thing was to fill my conscious mind with the presence of God. So I affirmed that reality in a present tense kind of way and kept affirming it. I took a phrase that expressed this and said it silently or out loud over and over again—"Father, I turn to you and fill my mind with your presence. Thank you that you are with me now..."

One thing led to another and I began to emphasise that fear does not come from God. He has not given us a "spirit of fear but of power and of love and soundness of mind"[2] and, "love casts out fear".[3] Instead of affirming fear, which was what I had been doing up till then, I dwelt on the power and love and soundness of mind that He provided for me and wanted me to have. My affirmation went something like this—"Thank you that you want me to have these good things. I am drawing upon them now and believe it by faith."

The thing that helped me most was to praise God. Because I was depending on God; because He was giving me the power and love and soundness of mind; because what had been revealed to me was being put into practice, I praised God—"Thank you Father, thank you Jesus, thank you Holy Spirit. Thank you for what you have done for me on the Cross, thank you for what you are doing for me now. Praise God, praise God, praise God."

Sometimes a problem came into focus that was so much a problem that I was unable to turn to God. However great the need, however much the effort, I came back to affirming the difficulty and being swamped with self-pity. I exhausted prayer, and prayer exhausted me. When this happened, there was no alternative but to let the problem ride. At a later time I would return to it again and find that my prayer reaction was the more effective. It was as though the earlier prayer effort had taken me along the road some distance, despite having to stop. When I started again it was from the previous stopping place so that further progress was made. Even

2   2 Timothy 1:7
3   1 John 4:18

so, exhaustion point could be reached again. But, if I persevered, I found that in the long run I could again react to any mountain in the positive way I have described.

As I came to this inner reality of depending on God and getting it right (if not every day, certainly in a general way) two things happened as a result. The first, and most important, was that the Holy Spirit showed me more of what God was like. Words cannot convey what this meant. All that can be said is that it was a new and wonderful experience of being guided into the Truth. The things that were highlighted were especially to do with the holiness of God and that it was my duty and privilege to draw on that holiness for myself and be made like Him more and more. It was both elevating and humbling to be ministered to in this way. This gracious work of the Spirit did not come to me every day but it came two or three times every week. One of the memorable aspects of this experience was its perfect development. It was a growth experience. Each revelation, if that be the right word, was complete in itself but was also a needful preparation for the next one. The next experience, when it came, built perfectly on what had gone before. An analogy, which is an imperfect one, is that it was like going on a journey and coming to a breathtaking view that had not been seen before. Then, turn the next corner and there is more …

This leads me to say that, at a later time, I realised that everything shown me was in the Bible. It took me some time to see this because it was all so new and different. I had read the Scriptures for many years and treasured their truth in my heart but can only say that when the Holy Spirit makes the Truth to be Truth it is as if you had never heard it before.

The second thing that happened was that my lifelong problems began to disappear. This part was not so easy to assess because as they disappeared I forgot what it had been like before! It was as though they had never been. When Jesus spoke of the mountain being cast into the sea it was a figure of speech that describes exactly what takes place. With me, the mountain was moved spadeful by spadeful over a period of three to four years; but moved it was and never to return. The only time those problems ever come to mind is when I deliberately recall them so as to give a testimony of what God can do when we draw on His help in an effective way.

At the time, I thought of these things as problems that were being worked through. It was only later I saw that my "dark night" with its good end result was an echo of what Paul the Apostle had himself gone through. It was fascinating to realise that as he worked through his own crippling difficulties he, too, was overwhelmed by them at first and only later saw their religious significance.

> *"We should like you, our brothers, to know something of what we went through in Asia. At that time we were completely overwhelmed, the burden was more than we could bear, in fact we told ourselves that this was the end. Yet we believe now that we had this experience of coming to the end of our tether that we might learn to trust, not in ourselves, but in God who can raise the dead. (2 Corinthians 1:8,9 Phillips)"*

The problems don't come from God; they come from Satan and the sin of the world. But they work together for good because God uses them to serve His good purposes. Paul said that the good they serve is to bring us to the end of our tether that we might learn to trust not in ourselves but in God. Although it had taken me a long time to get the message—and then only because of intervention from above—this was what I had begun to do. I didn't call it healing, but it was the foundation on which healing would later be built. More properly it could be called a theology of permitted difficulties.

As I got on top of my own permitted difficulties and grew in this scriptural understanding, to my surprise people began coming to me with difficulties of their own and wanting help. I was surprised because people had not sought me out before in this way and because my experiences had not so far been shared with others. My visitors just came "out of the woodwork". With hindsight I realise that God had sent them. He uses us according to our capacity to minister help and healing, and we comfort others with the comfort with which we have been comforted by God.

Not that I had any idea as to how to go about this but a knowledge of counselling procedures gave me a start. I accepted these people, listened and sought to understand. When it came to doing something to assist them I just told them what God had done for me. We were to learn from our difficulties so that we depended on God more. If they got that principle right then everything else would come right. Although the circumstances with which the folk came varied greatly, I found that, if they followed the guidelines that I have set out, they drew upon the same power with the same remarkable result. They increased in their experience of God, and in varying but meaningful degrees, left their presenting problems behind. In other words, this wasn't something for me only, but was for all those who would apply it in their own lives.

One thing more needs to be added. As my understanding of these things grew, I found the real need was to seek God for Himself. Even when we turn to God and depend on Him more, our pre-occupation can still be with ourselves and our pain and our burden. That is not wrong in itself, and is more than understandable. But if what has been said is to work in an optimal way, one has to come to the point of wanting God for Himself and not so that He will cast our burden into the sea.

No-one says it is easy; but if we set our heart to understand and grow in our capacity to do it we will ultimately want this more than anything else and rejoice in it. And, when that happens, the heavens open and we cannot contain the blessing He pours out. God is no man's debtor; if we seek His Kingdom and His righteousness first, then He meets our other needs as well, the Bible says.

Ultimately we should thank God for our problems because, without the motivation they give, we would never come to the good things that can be ours when we react in a positive and creative way. The strange truth is that through our permitted difficulties we come to the power of Christ, and by the power of Christ our mountain is moved. St. Paul summed it up superbly both for himself and for us;

"I will all the more gladly boast of my weakness that the power of Christ may rest upon me." [4]

Jim found ways to discipline his mind so as to be filled with something else—all the fullness of God. This became a spiritual journey that eventually overcame his fear even though it could, and would, so easily come back if he allowed a spirit of fear to get a foot in the door. He would refer to this as the "slippery slope" of his emotional dilemma. He clearly utilised his accumulated knowledge as he embarked upon a strict regime of prayer, combining his resources of mind and spirit to allow perseverance to have its perfect work so that he could be complete, lacking in nothing.[5]

As Jim continued to persist, the periods of relief lengthened, but he often said that it was a full-time job maintaining his focus. He coined the phrase, "Without so much as putting in a comma or a full stop", since he couldn't relax for a moment in his determination to exclude fear from his mind. As soon as he allowed a comma or a full stop, he was back on the slippery slope! But, the impossible had become possible. He was starting to come out of the wilderness!

AN ANECDOTE

On one particular occasion, at a small country church, Jim was teaching a group of people about Jesus calming the storm (Mark 4:37-39). The topic reminded him of a time when his house was being buffeted by a severe storm which was rattling the windows and blowing down trees and fences around his house.

It took him some time to realise that he could pray about this and take authority over the elements. So he prayed, believing, that the storm would cease and his home would be safe. He turned to face north, then south, east and west, holding his hands up against the storm, saying,

---

4   2 Corinthians 12:9

5   James 1:4

"In Jesus' name be still, wind, and blow no more." He said that the wind didn't stop altogether, but within the boundaries of his house it died down so that the windows stopped rattling.

As he told this story he went through the motions of holding up his hands in all four directions, repeating his command, "In Jesus' name be still wind, and blow no more."

At the end of his message they were to sing a hymn, but the organist couldn't raise a note from the organ—there was no wind! Jim said it was a most practical demonstration, and they all had a good laugh. God has a sense of humour too.

Left
Staff Sergeant
Alfred James Glennon
age 26 years

Right
Rev Jim Glennon
celebrating
Holy Communion at
St. Andrew's Cathedral,
Sydney Australia
age 35 years

Left
*Jim's father John
Kiltanon Glennon
on ANZAC Day 1948*

Right
*Jim as a Boy Scout
age 14 years*

34

4

Challenges

A GLENNONISM

*The Healing Ministry is not just going to the doctor
with Amen on the end!*

When Jim started work at the Cathedral he had a small Bible Study group of about six ladies. Jim's focus on studying the Bible at that time was to find out how God could help him with his problems. Consequently, the members of the group began searching for biblical texts to support this idea. They wanted to move past the stage of "studying" to the stage of "doing" and one can only assume that they decided to "pray" about these matters.

Jim said that, at the time he didn't know there could be any such thing as "divine healing" because his theological training had taught him that healing was not for today. It was for apostolic times and God had withdrawn this blessing!

It was during a residential ministry course at Gilbulla that he read Agnes Sanford's book, *The Healing Light* and upon his return to Sydney he approached the Dean and asked if he could start a Service of Divine Healing at the Cathedral. The Dean graciously agreed and on September 28, 1960 he conducted his first service.

It wasn't until Easter 1961 during Agnes Sanford's visit to Australia that he became really aware of healing as a ministry. Up until then he had his little service of Divine Healing going on with the ladies from his Bible study group. He said he never advertised and the congregation grew through word of mouth as people shared their testimonies of healing.

One of Jim's challenges was to extend himself beyond a perception of his own ability in a ministry sense—to think and act "outside the square". It was so easy to follow the normal and conventional methods of ministry.

He was quick to learn that, not only is there a right and wrong way to present the Gospel (or the Kingdom, as he put it), but, more importantly, there needed to be a balance. He was acutely aware that there were clergy in many denominations who conducted funerals and weddings, attended functions, and preached sermons based solely upon their own theological training. He said that his own theological training did nothing to equip him for pastoral care or, in fact, for any other part of ministry in a parish. This was learned on the run.

Probably because of his own experiences, particularly those that embraced the Healing Ministry, it was his opinion that many clergy went through their entire career simply fulfilling these duties and responsibilities. There is nothing much wrong with that, he would say, but where was the challenge? Jim himself knew he still had much to learn after ordination and three curateships—by which time he was on the Cathedral staff.

The congregation at the Wednesday night Healing Service started to grow, but it wasn't just the number of people attending which attracted the attention of the senior Cathedral staff. It was the inconvenience!

Well, it's okay to have a handful of people meeting in the Side Chapel on a Wednesday evening, but now they are wanting to expand into the Cathedral, use the organ, have all the lights on, have a verger on overtime to lock up after everyone!

Furthermore, these "Healing Ministry" people don't simply go home after a service—they want to stay on and talk, drink coffee and eat, and even pray! (It's called fellowship).

Jim clearly remembered the initial growth and all its pain, and he had certainly never intended filling the Cathedral to capacity so that the Healing Service became the single largest ongoing activity ever known in the Australian Anglican Church.

However, there was soon to be another challenge for him when the healings which had so wonderfully marked the beginning of the ministry, suddenly stopped! He couldn't explain it, since he said they were doing things in exactly the same way as always. Who could he approach with this problem? Due to a somewhat strained relationship with the then Dean, he didn't feel he would get any sympathy from that quarter. Jim said it was as if all his demons had returned to haunt him.

It just so happened that Agnes Sanford was in Sydney at that time—1961—and Jim decided to approach her for help. He made an appointment to visit her at her hotel, and after some discussion, she laid hands on him and prayed. After about 20 minutes Agnes declared, "This isn't working." Jim had to agree. In retrospect, we know it wasn't that God was not willing, nor that Agnes was not able—the problem was Jim. She then asked if he had been filled with the Spirit. Jim replied that he had been baptised in the Spirit and thought that was all that was needed to be a fulfilled Christian. She replied, "Then why are you having all these problems?" His response was, "That puts me between a rock and a hard place."

Agnes told Jim that there are two blessings of the Holy Spirit; the first is to be baptised in the Spirit, and the second is to be filled with the Spirit. She gave chapter and verse from the Bible in support of this, and explained that sometimes there were barriers to this second blessing because we build emotional walls around ourselves to protect ourselves from being hurt in relationships. Well, that struck a chord with Jim! Her discernment of his presenting circumstances was that he needed healing of the memories so that he could be open to receiving the Spirit. She prayed again. This time, Jim said, she prayed about situations in his past that only he knew about—even down to the colour of the wallpaper—and, as they were spoken out, he felt released, set free and eventually healed of all those latent memories.

The next time he met Agnes was in the Cathedral and she again offered to pray for him. This time she had barely opened her mouth when the floodgates opened, and Jim just knew the Holy Spirit was filling him because now he was an empty vessel and there were no blockages or barriers.

Jim said that Agnes Sanford was the most impressive woman he had ever met. Her discernment about things spiritual was beyond human understanding, and her belief in the Scriptures empowered her to achieve great things to the glory of God.

After that, the Healing Ministry took off and grew with ever-increasing numbers and healings, especially as the congregation was now involved in the laying on of hands. The Holy Spirit became a living part of the triune Godhead so far as the Healing Ministry was concerned.

At that time, and it is much the same today, the Diocese of Sydney was not known for its encouragement of the ministry of the Holy Spirit. This was one of the issues the then Dean disciplined Jim about. Jim said the Dean directed him never to speak about the Holy Spirit in the Cathedral, and he was obedient to this directive. This was not to say he agreed with the directive, but he was always aware of the tenuous nature of his position on the Cathedral staff and, in any event, he greatly valued and respected the authority of the Church. Perhaps it was not generally known that, contrary to the security of employment enjoyed by a parish minister (who cannot easily be dismissed from office, and usually then only if he were to have his licence revoked) Canon Jim's position was known as "locum tenens" which meant he could be dismissed in an instant, and apparently without justifiable reason. In all his 33 years of service he never enjoyed any security of employment on the Cathedral staff!

It was so important to Jim that Christians, as well as non-Christians, knew there was a resource available to help them and, more particularly, that the resource was within the Church — more importantly, that the place where thousands of people would find this help was the iconic Anglican Cathedral in the centre of Sydney.

Jim developed a strategy for his preaching at the Wednesday night services. He selected a theme about which he would teach during a given month. He wanted to encourage people in their knowledge of God and of the ministry of Jesus so that they would come back the following week to get the next installment. He would do this for three weeks and, on the fourth week, would often invite another clergyman to preach. He said he always had people giving their testimonies, since it demonstrated continual blessings from God.

Jim's style was unusual. He would typically start by sharing a personal experience, often of his own failure, and then tell the congregation how he dealt with that failure.

These personal experiences were common to all, and readily understood by everyone. He always referred to a person's unique situation (the point of felt need) as the "presenting circumstances". Later, he would simply refer to it as "the problem".

Then he would draw parallels from the Scriptures such that the congregation could apply the teaching to themselves, as well as understand the story. Other teachers, not necessarily in the healing ministry, start with a Scripture reading but, because these events happened 2000 years ago, their hearers tend not to understand the significance of the message for today. Congregations may also have been told that healing, as described in the Bible, was only for apostolic times. The attempt to explain the Bible like this—reading a passage and giving a verse-by-verse explanation—is not as effective as the way Jim taught. He was unique in this regard, doing the absolute opposite to what most everyone else did. I have rarely heard other clerics open their heart with stories of personal failures as a preliminary to scriptural enlightenment. He had moved outside the square.

AN ANECDOTE

By the mid-1980s the Healing Service dominated the weekly events at the Cathedral. One had to get there about an hour before the service started to get a seat, and at that time the Cathedral took about 750 people. There was a mixture of people in that total number, and Jim said it was about a third of core believers who prayed for others, a third of people who regularly attended, who wanted to believe, and would be prayed for, and a final third which he called transient. This final third came, didn't return regularly, and eventually drifted away. It was a friend of Jim's, whose name I cannot recall, who said to him one day, "You know what you've got here Jim," referring to the congregation, "you've got a shandy!" For the uninitiated, a shandy is a mixed drink of lemonade and beer. His point was, I believe, that when you've got a shandy you've got something different from what you really want. In other words it's diluted. If the whole congregation were believers, what a powerful and effective ministry it would be, but when you've got a shandy the believers get watered down, so to speak, so that the lemonade has the effect of reducing the power of the beer.

Testimony – Tony Mullins

J enny and I met Tony Mullins during our cancer ministry at
Golden Grove. Tony had already been healed when we met
but, as he was to learn, more challenges were ahead of him
and more healing was to happen. This testimony is based on that
which was published in the Healing Ministry Newsletter of July
2005. Having heard Tony's testimony at first-hand on a number of
occasions, I can now include details which, due to lack of space,
were omitted from the Newsletter.

When we first met Tony we knew nothing of his background, his
presenting circumstances, his causative factors as the Canon would
put it. So we were simply meeting him at his point of felt need.

Tony's journey with the Lord began about 20 years ago when he
was in St. Vincent's Hospital with liver disease due to alcohol abuse.
He had lost his job as a senior manager in his company, and his
wife and two children had left him. They had not simply walked
out—they loved him but were unable to cope with the regular
abuse which in its various forms, accompany the alcoholic.

Unless one has experienced alcoholism in a family situation it is
hard to appreciate its effects on the lives of everyone involved. In
no way were any members of Tony's family to blame; we have to

understand that at such times people get to the end of their tether and can't cope any longer.

At St. Vincent's Hospital Tony was lying in bed, his abdomen already marked out for surgery. One can only imagine his despair in such circumstances, quite apart from his addiction to alcohol. On the wall at the end of the ward was a Cross with a statue of our Lord. Tony was attracted to it, more and more, until one day he said, "I have had enough of this world. I am at the end of the road. I'm sorry for my stupidity. Are you really there Lord, and will you help me?" The response was immediate: "Yes, I am here, I have been waiting for you to call."

Over the next few weeks Tony began to read the Bible for the first time and to begin to pray. His liver condition improved, and doctors were so amazed and encouraged at the rapid repair of the liver cells that he was discharged — with strict instructions never to drink alcohol again.

Tony made a covenant with God that he would give up alcohol and give to Jesus the life Jesus had restored, to do with as He saw fit. Three months later his wife and children returned home. Twelve months later he started a new job and within five years the Lord returned him to a senior management position.

It would be nice if the story were to end here but, as Tony was to find out, it was only the beginning. He says, "I had repented, believed, but did not persevere with the most important aspect of the trilogy — obedience."

Due to work-related stress he suffered a nervous breakdown. The Lord had once again allowed him to come to the end of his tether, for His glory and for Tony's learning. It was at this time that he heard about the Healing Ministry at St. Andrew's Cathedral and began to attend regularly. Within four weeks he had recovered and was back at work, subsequently to be promoted to number two in his company later that same year.

Canon Glennon could be blunt and Tony needed his classic teaching in regard to not being problem-centred — to turn around 180 degrees was yet another lesson to learn.

Jenny and I invited Tony to do a teaching session during our residential cancer weekends and he took one of the sessions where we introduced what the Canon referred to as "cause and effect".

This session was called "The Primary". Tony spoke of the primary cause of sickness as being the stress brought about by a person's unique circumstances. His was alcohol. He told of a situation during a family row where he ran down the hallway to get out of the front door—with saucepans flying after him. It would have been funny if it were not so desperate. As he slammed the front door behind him he shouted, "Wow, have you got a problem!" He later realised that it was he who had the problem!

There were to be other tests to his faith except that now he not only knew where to go for help but was equipped through the outreach of the Healing Ministry for the next hurdle of his journey with Jesus. A routine check revealed a dark mole at the base of his neck which turned out to be a spreading malignant melanoma. He went into hospital for exploratory surgery at St. Vincent's Hospital to see how far the thing had gone into his system.

The first person Tony spoke to about the cancer, apart from the doctors, was a lady at the Healing Ministry and with her prayers and a very positive attitude he again called upon the Lord for help. This time, and now it was no great surprise to him, he received the reply, "I am always here to help you; you only have to ask." And, praise God, the next operation revealed no sign of the cancer, which had reached to within one centimetre of his lymphatic system.

It would have been at this time that Tony called us and asked for prayer. As number two in his company there was a certain amount of entertaining involved. This was to test him, as entertaining involved that dreaded alcohol. He could not refuse invitations but, worse still, the CEO would encourage him to have a drink. "One little drink won't hurt you," he would say, and the pressure increased. Tony's request for prayer was that God would stop this incessant pressure from the CEO, and he didn't care how He did it.

God doesn't always answer our prayers in the way we might think, and the outcome was certainly not our specific prayer, neither was it Tony's suggestion. The CEO resigned and the position was advertised Australia-wide and overseas.

Tony's next prayer started with praise and thanks for past blessings and went on, "Lord if you want me to be appointed CEO you will give it to me and I will do it with all my might to the glory of the Lord who gives it to me!" Many interviews ensued and Tony got the job; moreover, he was to become the longest serving CEO of the company.

Another of Tony's challenges was when he had another melanoma scare. At the doctor's surgery the medico told him he had some bad news! "You have a very bad case of arthritis." Tony raised his hands heavenward and said, "Praise God for arthritis." Well, it wasn't cancer!

Tony later served as a member of the Cancer and Chronic Illness Support Team and, at the time of writing, is a Director and the Acting Chairman of the Board of Directors of the Healing Ministry Centre Golden Grove Ltd.

5

The Postal Congregation

A GLENNONISM

*We only remember about 10% of what we hear,
so if what I have to say today is important to you
(and it may save your life), take notes!*

In the early days of the Healing Ministry there was a deaconess who attended the services and who became a part of the Healing Ministry staff, even occasionally preaching. Her name was Deaconess Gwyneth Hall, and she was a believer in what the Bible refers to as, *"Whatever you ask"* (Mark 11:24). Almost from the outset she took written notes of Jim's Wednesday evening sermons and typed them up, using carbon paper to produce multiple copies. This was in the days before photocopy machines and word processors. Jim didn't miss a thing and, one day, asked her what she was doing. Gwyneth explained that she had a few friends who couldn't get to the Cathedral every Wednesday and she wanted to give them the next installment so they didn't miss anything. Jim suggested that, to make things easier, he should buy one of those new-fangled cassette tape recorders so she wouldn't have to write so fast. She could record the sermon and then take the cassette home and type at leisure. This she did.

As Gwyneth posted these sermon notes out each week, the number of people wanting them increased to the point that she was forced to make more and more carbon copies. So the Healing Ministry bought a Roneo machine to produce multiple copies. Gwyneth had now moved from a handful of sheets to a few hundred sheets. She worked out that it was more cost-effective to print a sermon on each side of the paper and do a posting every four weeks instead of every week. It developed, therefore, into a monthly posting of four sermons on two sheets of paper.

As the ministry grew at the Cathedral, so also did the postal distribution, and the people "out there" were soon referred to as the Postal Congregation. Gwyneth communicated with many Postal Congregation members and it became a ministry in its own right. It was not long before these notes were going overseas and the ministry was recognised worldwide as being able to meet the needs of people wherever they might live, through believing prayer. This introduced a new awareness of intercessory prayer and, in the same way that people attending the Cathedral services were prayed for and received blessing, so also did people in far away countries. Prayer was no longer something that required attendance in person at the Cathedral.

Because of the growth in the Postal Congregation it became necessary to request a contribution towards postage and printing. Gwyneth developed a system of costing which depended upon how many copies were posted, to which State in Australia or country overseas, and on the method of mailing—first or second class airmail, surface mail or parcel post, etc.

A friend of the Healing Ministry set up a computerised data base to record the names and addresses of people receiving the sermon notes, plus details such as the amount of their subscription and when they had paid. This programme also printed the labels, greatly assisting in the preparation of sermon notes distribution. It became quite complex because many Postal Congregation members didn't just send their post and packing costs—they sent a donation as well. The blessings flowed in both directions.

There were people receiving 50, and others 100 copies, for distribution within their own churches. At its peak we were printing between 5,000 and 7,500 copies, most of which were posted, but some were distributed at the Cathedral so that, if people missed a week, they could catch up on Jim's teaching. Also, at its peak, these notes were being posted to 36 countries overseas as well as all over Australia, and a team of helpers was needed to assist Gwyneth. It was, and still is today, an incredible ministry by any standard.

The feedback from recipients of the sermon notes was encouraging, to say the least. There were Bible study groups which used the notes as a basis for study, reflection, and prayer. Some Postal Congregation members would say that they could always tell when the sermon notes were delivered to their rector by the quality of the sermon the following Sunday.

A committee of which I was a member, and Gwyneth the Chairperson, was formed to administer the Postal Congregation. We were accountable to the Leaders Committee which was responsible for all aspects of the Cathedral Healing Ministry. Each year the Postal Congregation Committee organised a residential seminar specifically for country and overseas members who wanted to come to Sydney and gain first-hand experience of how to draw upon the blessings of God. Typically there were about 20 to 30 people, and they came mainly from interstate and New Zealand, and sometimes from Third World countries. Such overseas visitors were often clergymen-in-training who could not afford the costs associated with travel and accommodation. The "stand alone" Postal Congregation financed these visitors. Seminars were held at Vaughan College, Eastwood.

The Postal Congregation was subsequently very supportive in purchasing the Healing Ministry Centre at Golden Grove in Newtown, Sydney, giving generously towards its acquisition so that no mortgage was taken out—but more of this later.

The Postal Congregation still maintains a supportive role in ministry as well as financially. Latterly, sermon notes have been distributed by electronic mail. Some notes are still posted but the numbers have decreased. There are now a number of other healing ministries in local and interstate churches whereas, when the Healing Ministry began at the Cathedral, there were virtually no other healing services being conducted.

AN ANECDOTE

It was amazing that Jenny and I had to go half-way around the world to learn about the Healing Ministry at St. Andrew's Cathedral and to be given Jim's books to read. Back in Australia, Jenny's first encounter with Jim was at Golden Grove, where he was conducting a seminar. She hung on to his every word. When he had finished, a lady sitting towards the front spoke up, "Canon, can I ask a question?" Jenny was astounded by Jim's prompt and rather aggressive response, "No, you may not!"

We subsequently learned that this particular lady had attended just about every presentation Jim had given at the Centre and elsewhere, always arriving late and always trying to ask questions that could have elicited the response, "I've been telling you that for the last hour—weren't you listening?" Jenny overcame her initial shock as she came to know Jim better, and also the lady in question.

6

The Healing Ministry Centre Golden Grove Ltd

A GLENNONISM

*We have to search the Scriptures
to find what God has provided.*

A t the end of 1960, the Healing Ministry booked Gilbulla, a residential Christian retreat centre southwest of Sydney, for the whole holiday period up until January 31, 1961. People came for however long they were able—some for a few days, some for the entire period. Jim noticed, however, that people who came for a few days benefited more than they would have done by simply attending a Wednesday night service at the Cathedral.

Because of the blessings received, as well as the popularity of the exercise, the Healing Ministry held a similar residential retreat at the end of the following year and also on the ANZAC Day weekend. This pattern was repeated for the next 11 years.

Then, in 1971, Elizabeth and Arthur Daikin rented a facility closer to the Cathedral. It was half a house (actually the downstairs half of a duplex) right on the beach at Collaroy, on the northern beaches of Sydney. At first, this was for a three-month period, later for eight or nine months of the year.

Jim gave credit to Beth (as she was known) who, together with her husband, organised the whole thing so that Jim only needed to be involved with the spiritual aspect. Again, Jim could not help but notice that people were blessed much more during these periods of fellowship in residence than during a service that lasted a little over an hour.

He didn't work out the reason for this until he asked a colleague who was passing through Sydney, the Rev Stanley Giltrap. Stanley came from Ireland, and was with the Church Missionary Society [CMS], working with the East African Revival Fellowship [EARF]. He told Jim that EARF emphasised the verse 1 John 1:7, the first part of which reads: "... *if we walk in the light, as he is in the light, we have fellowship one with another..."* (KJV). He put the question to Jim, "Why is this so?", and said that the rest of the verse gives the answer. It is because, "... *the blood of Jesus Christ, his Son cleanseth us from all sin"*. Therefore, Stanley said, the EARF was mindful of the need to have Christian fellowship with someone *every day*! This confirmed Jim's view that it was much easier to do this in a residential facility than in the more formal and structured Cathedral environment.

In late 1984 the Daikins had to give up the ministry at Collaroy because of their advancing years. The leaders of the Healing Ministry started to look around in earnest, and pray for their own "Gilbulla", but nothing seemed to be available. In December 1984 they reached crisis point. At their meeting on a particular Thursday evening, the view was expressed that they should stop looking for a "Gilbulla" — a place in the country — and start looking for a place in the city. Jim was disappointed, since he had always had in mind a Gilbulla-like place, and he felt that one always got more for one's dollar the further one got away from the city. Nonetheless, he acted on consensus; the meeting had decided that this is what should be done, and he agreed.

The following Monday, one of the leaders, John Davis, went to a local real estate agent. Jim used to describe John as a person who could "nose around", and as someone who "didn't sit around here; he was moving around out there".

John told the agent what he was looking for, and the agent's response was that a property named "Golden Grove", which fitted the description, had come on the market that very day! It was a large property, consisting of a gentleman's residence, to which the owners, the Sisters of Mercy, had added a commercial kitchen, an auditorium, a chapel and a four-storey extension with some 30 bedrooms. It stood on three-quarters of an acre—and it was in the city. The Sisters of Mercy had recently been leasing it out since they no longer had need of it. Then they decided to liquidate the property to help finance another area of their ministry. The asking price was $850,000.

The other leaders were notified, and inspected the property the next day. One of them remarked, "This is Gilbulla in the City". Jim's own reflection was that he had always wanted something that was set up by the Catholics since they knew how to do things properly, such as having a chapel, and a high wall around the property for privacy. They always had an eye for a "good position"; it seemed that everyone was happy with this choice.

For those with a historical bent, the following information, researched by Dorothy Bird, will be of interest:-

The land on which the property called "Golden Grove" stands is a portion of a grant of 240 acres granted to William Bligh in 1806. The grant was known as Camperdown Estate and was located on the highest point between Botany Bay and Sydney Harbour. This Estate stretched from Wilson Street across City Road down to Parramatta Road in Camperdown, then in a northerly direction down into Annandale, ending at Johnstone's Creek near the present Johnstone Street, Annandale.

Various subdivisions of the land in Bligh's grant and changes of ownership of the different parcels of land would have taken place between 1806 and 1870 until, some time before August 1870, Edward Mason Hunt became the owner of an area of slightly over two and a half acres bounded by Newtown Road (City Road),

Queen Street, Wilson Street and Forbes Street. He purchased this portion of the grant for seventeen pounds. In 1874, having by then had the land converted from the original Old System title to Torrens Title, Hunt subdivided it and sold part of it (an area of almost one and a half acres bounded by Newtown Road, Queens Street, the southern boundary of what is now the Golden Grove property and Forbes Street) to Edward Chisholm.

In 1877 Chisholm subdivided again and sold the Golden Grove property (an area of slightly less than three-quarters of an acre) to Lovett. In 1893 the property was passed to Davies, and in 1896 to Moran and others, in 1913 to Kearney and others, and in 1953 to the Trustees of the Sisters of Mercy (Parramatta)—and in 1985 to the Healing Ministry Centre Golden Grove Limited.

It is understood that Edward Chisholm erected the original house in the 1870s. The house was described as a Georgian-style gentleman's residence, and boasted a tower which gave views to the waters of Botany Bay. The tower was later demolished and replaced by a pitched roof. The residence was named Mount Eagle and an eagle with outstretched wings was mounted on a rocky crag and stood at the entrance gates. Two carved lions kept guard from a vantage point in the garden.

An architect who resided in Forbes Street came to look at Golden Grove a few years ago, and it was his opinion that the original entrance was at the side of the house where carriages would be able to drive through the main gates and stop at the foot of the steps to the verandah.

Dorothy believes the two lions now positioned each side of the front steps were originally perched at each side of the entrance at the side of the house which was then the main entrance. Certainly the records show that the front porch was added to the original house when the additions were made.

The next step for Jim was to contact a friend, Sir Harold Knight, who was, before his retirement, an adviser to the Reserve Bank of Australia. No good having friends in high places if you don't use them from time to time, was Jim's comment. Sir Harold came out straight away and viewed the property. His first remark was, "You're taking a big bite of the cherry Jim." His next was more encouraging, "Where can we have a council of war?" Jim invited him back to the Cathedral and the matter was discussed further. The next thing to do was to take legal advice.

In an ongoing process of protocol, Jim went to see the Archbishop and the Chapter, as well as the Dean, telling them that a holding deposit needed to be placed by Friday of the same week! One can only imagine what went through the minds of the hierarchy when this suggestion to purchase such a large property was tabled. There have been a few embellished stories about them saying in effect, "No way", or that they would have nothing to do with this financial millstone. Certainly they were not prepared to foot the bill, neither were they prepared to act as guarantor should there be a mortgage taken out. In actual fact, what they said was that the Healing Ministry could go ahead, conditional upon two things:

1. *Provided that the Healing Ministry has 2/3rds of the asking price in cash or pledges by the time contracts are to be exchanged — January 31, 1985;*

2. *That ownership of the property is to be in the name of a company and nothing to do with the church.*

In other words, you have about 30 days to raise the money yourselves, and if anything goes wrong it mustn't fall back on the Chapter or the Cathedral to bail you out. The impression given was something along the lines of, "You've got Buckley's chance", meaning no chance at all.

On Friday of that week the Healing Ministry put down a holding deposit to secure the property, committing itself to exchange contracts on January 31, 1985. On the very next day, a Saturday, a Roman Catholic organisation approached the real estate agent, wanting to acquire the property, but was told that it was effectively off the market — at least until January 31. The person making the enquiry was amazed, as the organisation had been told a few days previously that it had only just come on the market.

The next step was to engage the help of the Healing Ministry and Postal Congregations, inviting donations in the form of cash or pledges. Naturally, prayer was a part of this very important period, both before, during, and after all the fund-raising activities. Jim said as an adjunct to the invitation, "Don't give what you can afford—we shall never get the money. Ask God how much you should give." He prayed about his own offering, asking God how much he should give and, to his astonishment, God said, "$10,000". Jim protested that he didn't have that amount, and the Holy Spirit replied, "You did not ask me how much you had, you asked how much you should give." Consequently, he had to sell some of his possessions, but gave the amount which the Holy Spirit had nominated. He said that two weeks later his brother, who was not a Christian, sent him a cheque—for no apparent reason—for his own use. It was for $10,000!

There was to be a special Giving Service, and people were asked to put their donation in the form of cash or a pledge into boxes as they came into the Cathedral. Some people gave $10 some $1,000 and some $10,000. After the service the money was counted, and it was $130,000 short of the required two-thirds. Then Jim asked his secretary, Pat Read, if she would just check the boxes to see if there were any more donations deposited on the way out. When she returned, and the boxes were emptied, they counted the sum of exactly $130,000. They now knew for sure that God was in it!

As a consequence, contracts were exchanged, and the Healing Ministry then had another six months during which to raise the balance. They did this in a slightly different way. At one stage Jim stood on the steps of the Cathedral handing out $5 and $10 notes. The idea was for people to take $5 and make it into $10, or take $10 and make it into $20 or $50 by buying materials like cake ingredients, and selling the cakes for a profit. The money rolled in. Two small boys set up a hot dog stand in the Chapter House on Wednesday evenings. They were completely self-sufficient with a large saucepan for hot water, rolls, tomato sauce, mustard and, of course, frankfurters. From their $10 talent money they raised $1,000. Another fund-raising activity was a variety stall started by Mary Verco, the wife of Peter Verco who was the organist for the Wednesday night services (it actually operated for about 12 years, continuing to raise money for the Healing Ministry). Jim said these were the happiest six months of his life.

Golden Grove was duly purchased, and Jim encouraged several ministries and activities there. It quickly became a place of worship and fellowship. There were teaching seminars, healing missions, and outreach meetings. Members of the Healing Ministry congregation would go in for the day and have a meal with others of like mind and spirit. The Cathedral was the focal point for the Healing Ministry itself, but at every Wednesday night service the activities for the coming week at Golden Grove were announced.

Another activity held at Golden Grove was the cancer ministry of which Jenny and I were leaders. We would have between 20 and 40 cancer people, and their carers, in residence from Friday afternoon until Sunday evening. In those early years, Canon Jim Glennon did our teaching and celebrated Holy Communion at the conclusion of the weekend. This went on for about ten years and, when Jim had other appointments which prevented him from attending, he trusted us to present the teaching. On such occasions he would phone us on the Sunday evening to enquire about the weekend's ministry and to give encouragement.

From this one might suppose that we simply drew attention to the next cancer weekend during preceding weeks at the Cathedral and people would flag their intention to come—not so! Jenny would be on the phone inviting people who would make all the excuses under the sun why they couldn't come. Even those who said they would, changed their minds several times during the weeks leading up to the weekend. I so clearly remember a young lady who came to the Cathedral the Wednesday before the cancer weekend she was due to attend. Her medical team had given her a life expectancy of three months. She said she was unable to come to the weekend because she was going to a BBQ!

God always provided the right number of beds for attendees even when, on occasion, there was no bed for us, or for some of our support elders, and we had to sleep under the Board Room table. All cancer people and their carers had a bed. One weekend, however, we were only half full and no amount of phone calls from Jenny could change the situation. At a human level we wondered what was going wrong and started the weekend in a state of nervous apprehension. However, we were soon to learn that God was still in control, because the needs of those attending exhausted our resources so much that we could never have coped with a full house.

Other activities included residential weekends for Inner Healing and Wholeness. Whereas the cancer ministry involved life-threatening situations, the Inner Healing and Wholeness weekends were more for physically well people who, nonetheless, benefited from emotional and spiritual healing. Whatever the felt need, the solution was ministry, leading to wholeness.

Seminars on all aspects of healing were available. People would come from the country and stay over to take advantage of Christian fellowship and ministry. Jim drew attention to Golden Grove as an outreach ministry, but emphasised the importance of the Wednesday night service at the Cathedral as being the place where people could come to know of the resources available—in other words, what God has provided.

The Cathedral was, therefore, integral to the life of Golden Grove. A word of explanation—the term "Cathedral" here refers to the Head Office of the Anglican Church in the Diocese of Sydney, Australia; the "Healing Ministry" held at the Cathedral is the service conducted by the Healing Ministry, a body operated by a Committee of Leaders; The Healing Ministry Centre Golden Grove Ltd, is an independent entity owned by the congregations of the Healing Ministry and operated by a Board of Directors. Few of those attending either facility knew, or even cared, about the legal distinction between the Cathedral and Golden Grove, and why would they? St. Andrew's Cathedral became identified with both the Healing Ministry and with Golden Grove.

One amazing aspect of the relationship between the Cathedral and Golden Grove was the lack of financial accountability between the two administrations. I mentioned earlier that Jim Glennon was not under any contract of employment, and was there as locum tenens. This carried over to his successor. When, fairly recently, the Chapter was under some financial stress, it sought to relieve its burden in part by dismissing him—virtually an overnight dismissal. There seemed to be a feeling that the Healing Ministry was a financial burden the Chapter could do without—they had not taken into account the offertories regularly given to the Cathedral by the Healing Ministry over many years. These monies were not registered as specific income and were entered into general revenue at the Cathedral. To make a case, the Leaders of the Healing Ministry pointed out that, quite apart from the Leader's quite considerable contribution to Cathedral staff activities, the Healing Ministry provided his accommodation, car and other expenses, and had contributed in excess of $2.5 million in offertories between 1965 and 2002. In other words, the Healing Ministry was an asset not a liability. The decision was rescinded!

AN ANECDOTE

Jim was the guest speaker at the 20th anniversary of the Healing Ministry Centre at Golden Grove. He told the audience that Sir Harold Knight, early in the establishment of Golden Grove, had made the observation that, "Things are all right now, but one day a headless monster will want to take the Centre over!" Some 18 years after the acquisition of the Centre, the then directors who, to my knowledge were unaware of Sir Harold's remark, considered this question. The property was by this stage valued at between $7m and $10m Australian, and the Articles of Association decreed that, in the event of liquidation for any reason, the assets would revert to the Chapter. Bearing in mind the events leading up to the acquisition of the property, the directors and shareholders convened an Extraordinary General Meeting at which this Article was changed. It was voted unanimously that, in the event of liquidation for any reason, the assets would revert to the Canon Jim Glennon Healing Ministry Trust details of which are presented later.

7

Dealing with
the problem-centred

Get up and turn your chair around 180 degrees.

Jim realised, very early in his ministry, that people's needs—their presenting problems—reflected the way in which they had dealt with their experiences in life. He also realised that, in spite of the difference in each person's experiences, the answer to their problems was the same—the promises of God, available through repentance and faith. Furthermore, the major ingredient in repentance was the need to forgive.

Over the years, Jim formed the opinion that the longer people talked about their problems, the longer it was before they were healed. He was neither inconsiderate nor dispassionate about their needs, but he did want to lead them out of bondage to their problem, so they could be free to accept God's healing.

Jim would often comment that certain people loved to hold on to their problems, even their sickness. One classic case he shared was that of a gentleman who came to see him for an hour every week for 18 months. There had been discussion at these meetings, and prayer, but one day the man said to Jim, "Today I'm going to tell you what my real problem is." Jim used this example to explain that the man had lived with his problem for 18 months, unhealed, simply because he hadn't got around to being absolutely honest about his presenting circumstances. When the problem was out in the open, appropriate prayer was administered and God was able to give His perfect blessing.

Jim's response to those who wouldn't stop talking about their problem was, "Stop telling me your problems or I will tell you mine; you don't want to know my problems, I assure you."

He would pose the question, "What do we do when we have a problem—let's say it's cancer, for example? What we do is to think about cancer every moment of the day, all its implications and consequences. We worry about the mortgage, the job, and the kids' education. In the short term, we worry about cooking the next meal, doing the washing, and the housework."

His method of dealing with this difficulty was to ask the person concerned to imagine him or herself to be sitting on a chair facing the problems. "If you are a Christian," he would say, "God is there behind you and your problems are in front of you. Now," he would say, "get up and turn your chair around 180 degrees so that God is now in front of you. Your problems are still there, but now they are behind you, and if they start to creep around the corner—push them back. Keep your focus upon God, because in God is the solution, the answer, the healing."

In his later years Jim became less tolerant of people talking about their problems; some were put off by his directness. However, he was just trying to get their attention focused correctly so as not to waste 18 months or so before moving from being problem-centred to solution-centred—focused on God.

During ministry times at the Cathedral, when there would be prayer made for people, with the laying on of hands, Jim would circulate and listen in on prayers in order to redirect anyone who was praying about the problem, or anyone coming for prayer who continued to talk about the problem. "You will never get your prayers answered like that," he would say. "Stop asking, asking,

asking God to take the problem away. God has already taken the problem away in the atoning death of Jesus who took upon Himself the sin of the world, our fallen human nature and our sickness and diseases."

Jim recognised the difficulties produced by problem-centred people. His reaction, when he saw a particularly difficult person, was to think, "Oh dear, here is that so-and-so person again that is forever talking about their problem." Even more insidious, he confessed, could be his reaction to the very thought of the person. "It doesn't matter," he would say, "whether I do this at every meeting or at every thought, or if I do it just once. It is the real me, reacting to the person's situation in a negative way."

He thought that such people would never be healed because of their inability to rise above their problems in the way in which he thought they should. But, whose fault was it? He acknowledged that the fault was his own:

Because I am holding them in bondage to their difficulty. Every time I think of them I am not believing for their healing, I'm believing they are a pain in the neck. This is the real me. It grieves me to acknowledge my shortcomings, not the least reason for which is that there have been occasions when I have failed to be obedient to God's word to the benefit of such people's healing. I have been disobedient and kept them in sickness. So unless you know the real me, perhaps you won't come to know the real you.

It is in our nature to hold our cards close to our chest. Another way of expressing this is to say that we all wear a mask and mostly pretend to be someone else, or else we build emotional walls around ourselves so that others don't see us as we really are. The expression we use to describe this situation is the "real me", the "real you", the "real us". If we do these things as a way of life, they become the "real us". God always knows who the "real us" is, even if we don't, so we are not fooling Him. The saying, "You can't fool all of the people all of the time" is not necessarily true. What is true is that we can't fool God at any time!

Whatever we think of, to the extent that we dwell upon it, perhaps even in our subconscious mind, that is the "real us". It might be the last thing we think of as we go to bed at night, or the first thing we think of as we awake. This is often the reason why things don't happen in answer to prayer. However, if we discipline ourselves to be Christlike, so *that* becomes the "real us", then we can experience the power of God in everyday life.

We used to have a session at our residential cancer healing weekends at Golden Grove called "open heart discussion". It was entirely confidential—radical stuff, and just as serious, emotionally, as the medical procedure of open heart surgery was physically. Interestingly, after this experience, most of the participants would say that they had never shared with another human being (or even God, for that matter) in such depth.

There is an extremely successful TV programme in the USA, also shown in Australia at the time of writing, called *Dr Phil*. It presents a secular worldview, nonetheless it has undertones of a spiritual nature. When Dr Phil was asked what were the most common questions people asked at the beginning of a session, he said that they had to do with relationships and the difficulties people experience in trying to communicate their feelings and emotional needs to others.

In the programme, Dr Phil asks people about themselves in order to get them to confront, not only the situation, but also their personal involvement in it. We could say he makes them identify with the *real* them. This is what Jim tried to get people to do, so as to experience the Kingdom.

After Dr Phil brings people to the point of confronting their problem with another person, he helps them change the way they are *reacting* to it—without trying to change the other person. We would call this "repentance". They would then be encouraged to say sorry to the other person involved, which of course we would refer to as "forgiveness".

Perhaps the most interesting aspect of Dr Phil's popularity is the vast viewing-audience which identifies with the needs and problems of others. This suggests we have a hurting population experiencing all sorts of relationship-based difficulties, which they are unable to deal with. This leads to divorce, alcoholism, gambling, drugs and violence. They are unable to deal with difficulties because they are not living a *real* life and they are not in touch with the *real* person

God created them to be, but try to be some other person they think the world finds more acceptable. Sadly, our churches should be the places they go to for guidance, but there are not many who teach these things — but Jim certainly did.

⟫◈⟪

AN ANECDOTE

Jim had a bee in his bonnet about people coming late to meetings. Mostly he could control his impatience and, while it upset him, he usually didn't address the offenders directly. At an appropriate time he would try and raise the matter in a reasonably polite manner — "Do you consider what I am saying to be important?", a rhetorical question. Without allowing time for anyone to reply, he would continue, "Because, if you do, then I would consider it a great act of courtesy if you would be here in time to hear it all." Occasionally, there would be someone who would attempt to justify his or her late arrival but this would just trigger an argument. Jim might say, "But it's always you who is late, and you have the shortest distance to come." On one such occasion he pointed an accusing finger at the offender saying in a loud voice, "Don't come late!", then he held up the flat of his hand as a means of dissuading any justification or excuse.

Canon Jim Glennon—approx 65 years of age

Left
*Canon Jim at
St Andrew's
Cathedral Healing
Service, pointing
"heavenward"*

Right
*Canon Jim Glennon,
Leader of the Healing
Service at St. Andrew's
Cathedral*

8

Retirement – of sorts

A GLENNONISM

Don't say 'but it's not working.'
Say, 'I believe it has happened. Thank you Father, by faith.'

When Jim retired from the Cathedral staff, he had been there for 33 years, 28 of which were as Leader of the Healing Ministry, and for all his opinionated theology, he had gained respect from the deans and archbishops. There were, inevitably, differences of opinion in matters of theology—the Charismatic Movement[6], for example—but he was always very loyal to his beloved Church, and sang the praises of all those in authority over him.

Both before and after his retirement Jim visited a number of churches by invitation, teaching in his unique way, but not everyone received his message. I guess it's not surprising. There were those who thought he was naïve, especially because he referred to

---

6   See Part Two "The Charismatic in the non-Charismatic Church".

drawing upon the healing power of God as being a simple thing to do. It was simple, but it wasn't easy! One had to accept biblical truths which are usually rationalised away.

He found greater acceptance of his teaching overseas, and accepted a number of invitations to speak at conferences and seminars in New Zealand, the United Kingdom and the USA. He often said that he was made most welcome and—while some of what he taught was challenged—on the whole he was accepted as an authority in his field.

When, soon after retiring, Jim received an offer of employment overseas, it came as quite a shock to him. The offer was made along these lines—"Jim, we would like you to come and minister in our Church. We will provide you with a house and a car and $100,000 a year." In Australia, clergy don't earn much, and they earned even less in Jim's day. His first thought was that he had always provided his own house and car, and never got anything like that sort of salary. So his response was to exclaim, *"How* much?" The person making the offer thought that he was challenging the figure as being too low, and quickly added, "We can make it more." Once the misunderstanding was sorted out, Jim expressed his appreciation but declined the offer, as he did not want to take on a new career, especially overseas.

When he was invited to teach at seminars, and was asked to nominate his fee, he always replied, "I don't have a fee, and I do not charge for my services." He always paid his own way—airline tickets and other transport expenses. What usually happened was that, after the seminars, there was a "love offering" and people gave generously in support of his ministry. This meant that he always came home having more than covered his costs. Suffice it to say that he never spent any of this money on himself.

He enjoyed his travels, and always spoke most appreciatively of people's generosity. He made many friends, and kept in contact with them over the years. Towards the end of the ten-year period during which he travelled—mostly to the USA—he became tired, and well he might, as he was then 75. He jokingly said his next book would be called, *The Beds I Have Slept In,* because he seemed to be forever changing locations and beds. Jim was a great dinner guest and was frequently asked to join an after-seminar meal with the organisers, but he had to be in the mood. He found this direct social interaction taxing, and would often retire early in order to escape.

He told me of a particular seminar he attended where, as usual, he was well received, except by one person — a medical doctor. One has to appreciate that sometimes Jim presented divine healing with such simplicity that the medical profession might well have problems accepting it. This doctor had probably spent nine years in training, followed by many years in practice. He had been unable to heal a patient's particular ailment — then Jim suggests that it could be done in an instant, because of what Jesus did 2000 years ago!

The doctor stayed behind after the teaching session and confronted Jim as he was leaving the hall. He introduced himself and asked, "What would you say if I said you were naïve?" The organisers of the seminar tried to whisk Jim away, fearing a long, verbal altercation. Jim turned to the man and replied, "I would say, *the foolishness of God is wiser than man's wisdom, and the weakness of God is stronger than man's strength.*" There was no further discussion, and the doctor was "gob-smacked".

Jim said later that this was a quotation from 1 Corinthians 1:25 and, although it was clearly in his memory somewhere, he had not needed to dwell upon the question and search his mind for the answer. It came to him in an instant and, as he walked away, he marvelled at his reply, thinking, *did I just say that?* Of course, Jim recognised the source, for which he gave glory to God.

Often he would phone me and ask, "Is it convenient to talk about a personal matter?" He was always so courteous, and wouldn't want to intrude. On one such occasion he wanted to talk about the possibility of moving into a retirement village. He had his name on a priority list at the Anglican Retirement Village facility at Woollahra in the eastern suburbs of Sydney. A unit had become available and, after some discussion, Jim asked Jenny and me to go and inspect it with him. He clearly wanted us to approve the idea of his moving, and there was no doubt it was a lovely unit with all the facilities he needed. However, this was not the issue; the issue was selling the family home.

Jim had lived in the same house in Clovelly for 83 of his nearly 85 years of life. It had been his parents' home which he had inherited along with all the furniture, as both his younger brothers had pre-deceased him. The furniture was, in his view, good enough for his parents, so it was good enough for him. The only piece of new furniture he bought for himself was his desk.

There is a rather general perception that, as we become older and more mature, decisions like this are made more easily because we draw upon our experience and maturity. This was not the case with Jim; he needed considerable support to even arrive at a decision to move. We played him at his own game. We suggested he should take his eyes off the problem (the house at Clovelly) and look to the solution (the unit at Woollahra), and prayed with him so that he would feel comfortable about the transition.

We also made the point that it was much better that he be involved in this decision while he was capable rather than wait until, perhaps, he became incapable, so that others would have to make the decision on his behalf. I am sure there were others whose opinion he valued, and doubtless he had similar discussions with them along the same lines. In any event, he decided to make the move. He put down an unconditional holding deposit on the unit. At the time, this was an act of faith since he had yet to dispose of his house at Clovelly.

His house was professionally marketed by a dear friend of his (a real estate agent) who had supported the Healing Ministry for many years, both spiritually and financially. It sold quickly. Jim would not accept the highest offer, preferring to accept a slightly lower offer from a young couple with a family. He had a great fondness for the young—by which I mean anyone under 30 years of age. He had an even greater fondness for children, and his attention to baptismal services, as well as his personal duties as Godparent, were exemplary. He had at least 52 Godchildren, all of whom he believed for, without a doubt in his heart, until they were able to stand in their own faith-position at confirmation.

Just on that point, I recall several occasions when people would approach him during a seminar with their concerns about the eternal welfare of their spouse or that of their children. People would bring this worry to Jim as "their problem", often irrespective of the context of his teaching for the day. Usually, they would ask Jim if he would talk to the family member about salvation because they had been so unsuccessful themselves. So this was their "Problem", which they brought to Jim.

In latter years Jim could be quite brusque in dealing with such requests, and say, "Well *you* believe for them". End of discussion! In moments of greater patience (or maybe I should say compassion) he would again refer people to Mark 11: 24 and the word that refers to us applying our faith for "whatever". Not only is this the way in which we can exercise faith for healing, but also it is our duty, or our commission, to do so for salvation. When he told people about all his Godchildren having been confirmed it was *his faith* statement—he was believing *for* them. So it is, when we would like our spouse or any other family member to be "saved", we simply stand in faith *for* them and continually believe for them. Of course, we can ask others to join us in this endeavour, and, if we have difficulty, then we can call the elders of the church to believe for the person concerned.

And so the great move to Goodwin House Anglican Retirement Village at Woollahra became a reality. Friends at the Healing Ministry helped him pack. He was ruthless in discarding many items that simply wouldn't fit in his much smaller unit.

There was a noticeable change in his lifestyle following the move. Prior to his relocation, Jim would regularly phone me to discuss issues that concerned him. We would talk over confidential matters for up to an hour or so. He was always very appreciative of these times but, after he moved, he no longer felt the need for them. I believe that a major reason for this was the companionship that was now available to him at the Village which, due to his bachelor status, he had never before experienced.

It used to embarrass Jim when couples hugged and kissed. Jenny's usual way of greeting him was with a handshake. Hence, she was most surprised on one occasion when we visited Jim in hospital, to hear him say—after we had been there for about two minutes—"You haven't given me a kiss yet!" After Jenny had "planted one on him" he said, almost in tears, "I wish I had a wife, Jenny." This was uncharacteristic of him, and perhaps his guard was down, but clearly he was reflecting upon his life and on opportunities missed.

Certain issues definitely exercised his mind as he tried to understand why people held certain views or opinions. One such issue had to do with family life. He would ask me, for example, why it was that particular parents always did so much for their son or daughter. "They are grown up now and should be standing on their own feet." I tried to explain that family is a very important part of life and we often do things beyond the apparent need to help, simply because they are family. This might be financial, or some other type of practical help. Jim seemed not to understand, and yet his own family was the Church (the Body of Christ) and, when someone had a need, he gave generously in support of that need in exactly the same way as any parent would do in support of their children.

And so, following the move to the Village, our phone conversations all but ceased, and I believe the issues that had previously concerned him when he had lived alone, paled into insignificance.

He already knew many of the residents before he moved in, and they embraced him in Christian love and fellowship. When I was attending to his furniture and effects following his death, people would tell me about their little chats with Jim in the garden. They said he might be reading the newspaper, or a book, but was always courteous towards anyone seeking his company.

AN ANECDOTE

It saddens me to say — and Jim shared this view — that "the world outside" is not simply the secular world. It can be the world inside the Church, where congregations believe for salvation but not for healing!

After Jenny was healed of cancer through the ministry at Golden Grove, she spent almost every day there because, as she put it, there was never a negative thought from anyone. But when we returned to our parish church, well-meaning members of the congregation would come up and ask how she was, inferring that she was on borrowed time. When she told them she was healed they would ask, "But how are you really?" as if she was trying to deceive them!

Whenever I attended church on my own, the same people would come up to me to offer their condolences, presuming that Jenny had died, because she wasn't with me. Others would cautiously enquire after her health. They seemed not to believe me when I told them she was very well, thank you. So, you see, both Christians and non-Christians can disbelieve the healing power of God, and this is just as wrong as not to believe God for all His "very great and precious promises". (2 Peter 1:4).

Testimony – Don Jaeger

—◆—

During the summer of 1992, I was diagnosed with ALS—Lou Gehrig's Disease, which is fatal. Well, thanks to God, His Son Jesus Christ and the Holy Spirit, I no longer have the disease. And thanks to Canon Jim Glennon of Australia for his selfless, God-centred leadership and teaching on Christ-based healing.

Of very special significance to me was the comment of Father David Wilson (Rector of All Saints Episcopal Church in Winter Park, Florida) and Canon Glennon's teaching that the disease is *not* the will of God. God wants us perfect. Disease is evil. I thus began to pray the Lord's Prayer of "deliver us from evil" with new fervour and meaning. God also instructed me to receive communion with Christ's Blood washing the "nerve horns" in my spine and His body strengthening and healing those "nerve horns".

In July 1992, two of the best experts in Central Florida, an EMG (nerve response test) specialist and a neurologist, agreed on the diagnosis. It was then that Father Wilson told me of Canon Glennon's mission. That night, and the next, Canon Glennon and Father

Wilson and other members of All Saints clergy and lay leaders laid hands on me and prayed for my healing. My first ever "religious experience" occurred when I felt a warmness and peace, leading me to be convinced that I would be cured. I was even ready to dispose of the total ankle-foot brace I was wearing.

I then began to study Canon Glennon's two books, "How Can I Find Healing?" and "Your Healing Is Within You" daily, along with the Life Application Bible. Also, I attended healing services each week at All Saints and went to physical therapy in an effort to slow the inexorable decline of my body. All sessions were devoted to God in thanks for His promise of healing.

As Canon Glennon, and good sense suggested, I continued to seek other qualified medical advice and I was recommended to see either Mayo Clinic or our University. I got an appointment with a professor of neurology at the latter, still believing and knowing I was cured. It's important to note during my entire sickness and then healing process that God blessed me with Divine Peace such as I've never experienced before and certainly never under such life or death stress. I'm sure that because of the extreme nature of my problem, I actually got out of God's way and let Him work His will in my life. It's a shame it took something of this magnitude to teach me a lesson that I've been trying to learn for years.

I continued to inform my family, clergy, office staff and church leaders and friends of God's happening in my life and the progress of His cure.

It was while in the professor's office, waiting for him with my wife, that God gave me an irrefutable sign that even someone as dense as I could recognise! My skin temperature rose rapidly and a total encompassing, utter peace came over my body, to the extent that my wife saw it and confirmed it.

I told her the tests were perfunctory and we were "out of here".

The professor kept telling me to be patient during the exam and appeared to confirm through physical inspection that I was cured. However, he ran another EMG and confirmed a diagnosis of ALS.

I told my wife, and then my office and clergy by phone, that I believed I was cured and time would prove it.

A month later, having continued my prayer and studying and asking for a sign that the "mustard seed" was growing, I was asked by some exercise therapy people to lift some weight with only my lower legs to establish a baseline for further exercises. With my lower leg weakened through muscle atrophy due to the disease, and with absolutely no strain, grimacing or hanging on to the handles, I lifted the maximum machine weight of 220 pounds! This word flew all over the Centre[7]. God had further revealed His cure to me!

Continuing good health management, I made an appointment at one of the few and best hospitals in the United States specialising in ALS, Cleveland Clinic. En route, I had an opportunity to visit at a convention over thirty companies we represent, sharing with them my illness and belief that God had cured me, but if I were wrong (to comfort unbelievers) that I'd organised my company to survive my death.

Well, to close a long testimony, Dr Mitsumoto and his associates extended my stay at Cleveland Clinic to two days, including three hours of EMG tests by two different doctors! He told me that 'people in Florida may not believe me, but I see over 150 cases of ALS a year and you neither have or show signs of ever having had ALS disease'.

Praise God. I threw away my brace and went snow skiing!

I'm now in the post-healing stage, sharing with people, have cut down on my work activities (I used to average approximately 60 hours per week with many weekends) and spending more time listening to God; for I'm sure He has something special He wants me to do. As a reminder of my illness, I still have a weakness and pain in my left leg and in my right hand, the first extremities to be attacked by the disease.

For a while after the healing, the devil attacked me and tried to intrude on my blessed experience. He did so mainly by attempting to instill fear that the healing wouldn't last or I didn't deserve it.

---

7   This was a fitness centre or gymnasium where he undertook an exercise regime to put his faith into action. This is what was so unique about Don. Whereas others would have waited until the healing was absolute before telling anyone, Don told everyone as his act of faith before healing appeared, which is why the news went around the Centre. It was so unusual.

Canon Glennon's books, especially *How Can I Find Healing?*, deals with fear and through God's help I no longer have that fear and don't fear fear.

Thanks to God for Christ's birth and death, so we may be healed and forgiven.

Donald C. Jaeger
President and CEO of Jaeger Corporation
Winter Park, Florida, USA

Note: A few years after his healing, Don, and his wife Sarah, visited Golden Grove to get first-hand experience of a residential healing ministry centre. The Jaegers worship at All Saints Church, Winter Park, Florida, where Don is Director of the Healing Ministry which was established as a result of Jim Glennon's visit and Don's subsequent healing.

9

A matter of life or death

A GLENNONISM

*It's no good simply knowing what God can do, or even
believing it for that matter (Satan knows and believes that).
We have to act upon it through repentance and faith!*

As previously mentioned, Jim would get very cranky if people arrived late for any of his seminar teaching sessions. He would often start after the scheduled time to allow for late arrivals. This was because his introduction would set the scene, so to speak, for the next hour or two and, if someone arrived late and missed this, the latecomer wouldn't understand his presentation. Another reason for him being upset by people arriving late was that it distracted him.

He wanted everyone to pay attention to what he had to say because he considered the teaching very important. For some people, it could be a matter of life or death! He never spoke from notes, and always prayed and thought his presentations through meticulously, interspersing what he had to say with anecdotes or biblical quotations. He would also discourage questions during his presentations because, again, they distracted him from his objectives.

Jim had many idiosyncratic ways of speaking when he gave talks. When he felt the need to emphasise a particular point he would say, "Do you see?" What he really meant was, "Are you listening to me?" or "Are you awake?" At other times he would be even more direct and say, "Don't tell me you do what I'm teaching, because you don't!" As one might imagine, this didn't go down very well and some folk got upset. It was usually the very people who *did* do what he said who got upset, and those who didn't were unaffected!

One of the things that got up Jim's nose, was the misuse of the term, "God's will". When used in his hearing in his own ministry, he would pounce on the phrase, even if it were spoken halfway through someone's prayer. If it was said in his hearing in someone else's ministry his hackles would rise but he would remain silent. He would respect the other leader's ministry, especially in the public arena. He would possibly approach the minister afterwards and seek to enlighten him or her, but this would depend upon a number of factors, not least of which would be their reputation, or their attitude towards the healing ministry.

He wanted people to come to each session in order to see the big picture—the whole of his teaching on a particular subject. "What is the point of attending only the second session of a three-part seminar?" he would ask. If a person heard only a part of what he had to say, he or she might go away with entirely the wrong impression. Sometimes he would say to participants, "If this is important to you then attend every session—your life may depend upon it."

It was always a surprise to him that, however much he taught people how to pray, most of them never put it into practice. On more than one occasion he told me that he felt he was banging his head against a brick wall in terms of people's willingness to trust God. One such situation involved a group of nuns who had came to him for teaching, followed by laying on of hands in prayer for one of their Sisters, who had cancer. Jim said they were very attentive during the teaching, and because of their biblical studies asked some very sensible questions. He spoke to them about believing prayer and then they laid hands on the Sister and prayed for God's healing power. As usual, Jim's prayer was an affirmation that the Sister had been healed—a faith statement—because of Jesus' substitutional atonement. Healing was to be accepted as *"the substance of things hoped for, the evidence of things not seen"* (Hebrews 11:1 KJV). He always taught the need to hold to this position—to rest in the finished work of Christ—irrespective of what human perception we might have about the sickness.

One might suppose this to be the end of the story, but, as Jim left the church, he came across the nuns in the car park. They were in a huddle, crying. Jim approached them, asking what was the matter now? They looked at him in surprise and said, "But our Sister is dying of cancer!" It was as if they hadn't heard a word he had said!

One of Jim's assertions was that the people who experienced the most difficulty in grasping his teaching were those who were already in the church, irrespective of their denomination. He thought that the reason for this was because they came to their point of felt need with all sorts of misinformation, whereas those who had absolutely no Christian background were a "blank page", and seemed more readily to accept what needed to be done. Jim referred to this misinformation as "churchianity".

The following is a note which I found in his personal papers after his death. It records an event which took place at the International Conference of the Order of St. Luke the Physician, held in Melbourne in 2002. The Conference consisted of 200 delegates—clergy from various denominations from the USA, Canada, the Bahamas, the United Kingdom and Kenya, as well as Australia and New Zealand. Jim wrote:-

The main papers of the Conference were given by three medical practitioners, one of whom was also a theologian, and myself. Bible studies were given by Archbishop Raynor who had been the Archbishop of Melbourne and Primate until his recent retirement. He gave Bible studies on three healing miracles in St. John's Gospel. These were edifying and valuable. The main Conference speaker was Emeritus Professor Radford who gave two papers and said that every church should have a Deliverance Ministry and a Healing Ministry and every clergyman should be trained so as to have a ministry that expressed the teaching and insights of the New Testament. While the other papers were very valuable mine was the only paper that explained what one needs to do so that healing is experienced in point of fact.

I also had two electives, which meant that delegates could choose between the half dozen electives provided. More than half the delegates to the Conference came to my elective, again because I explained to them what they needed to do to have healing, in point of fact. At the end of one of my electives I invited anyone to come forward and seek healing, and we then prayed for the leader of the American delegation who had had pain in her knees for about five years, and was in pain at the time. But when I invited those present to lay hands on her and pray the Prayer of Faith, the result was very disappointing indeed. People had no idea how to pray in faith and when I asked the person who was sick if the prayers had made any difference, she said that they had not, and that she was still in pain. I then led them in a prayer that was something like this — 'Father, we thank you for your promise of healing. We accept it for this your servant in the same way as we accept salvation. We now affirm that she is being healed and we believe it before we see it and we put our faith into action'. I then asked them to rest in the fact that she had been healed, and when I asked the lady concerned what had happened as a result of the prayer, she said that all the pain had immediately gone. I then asked her to do something that she had not been able to do before as a sign of her faith for healing and she said she could not kneel down. She then knelt down with no problem whatsoever. The Bible says 'You ask and receive not because you ask amiss'. We have to pray the Prayer of Faith as it is in the Scriptures, and show our faith by what we do, and then there will be an answer to prayer.

AN ANECDOTE

Let me tell you about a person who, Jim said, "had got it" and had "put it into practice". I shall call this person Michael.

79

He came to one of our cancer weekends when Jim was teaching. Michael was so advanced with cancer he was barely able to walk. During the teaching sessions, when everyone else sat on rather uncomfortable plastic chairs, Michael had to lie down on a sofa in the auditorium. The focus of Jim's teaching on this day was about the faith needed by the person praying rather than the person receiving prayer. At the end of the teaching, during question time, someone asked how much faith did the person being prayed for need to have in order that they be healed. Before Jim could reply, Michael croaked up from his sofa bed, "Well, Lazarus didn't have much did he?"

Michael had a great sense of humour, and recovered sufficiently to survive for another ten years. A year after his visit to Golden Grove, he took up Spanish dancing lessons! This was a guy whose spine was so affected with cancer he could barely walk before he came, and had to wear a back brace.

Michael lived interstate. On one occasion he rang to say he felt under attack spiritually and needed to get to Golden Grove for support and believing prayer. I met him at the airport. He was so weak he couldn't lift his suitcase off the luggage carousel. I carried his suitcase and drove him to the Healing Ministry Centre, very slowly, since every bump was painful. The period at Golden Grove rejuvenated him. I phoned him the week after his return home to see how he was. I couldn't raise him but left a message. He phoned back that evening to apologise for not being able to hear the phone—he had been in the garden mowing the lawn!

Michael often said he wished he had lived in Sydney where there were people who would continually believe for him. The Christians where he lived were good people but he felt that they simply didn't have the teaching to uphold him every day. His local pastor had once visited him and asked, "What can I do for you, Michael?", to which he replied, "You can stop praying for me and start believing for me." Michael said this went right over his rector's head. It was Jim Glennon's teaching, but Michael's personal situation had left him isolated from the Church—from the ministry of all believers. Nonetheless, he was grateful to God for those extra ten years, which were mostly fruitful and happy.

10

The Baby
and the Bathwater:
maintaining a balance

A GLENNONISM

Faith isn't just what we believe — it's what we do.

Those who knew Jim were aware that he drew upon many sources of information in his pursuit of balance in his spiritual pilgrimage. For those who didn't know him this could lead to misunderstanding.

For instance, without seeking to be critical, he would say that the Anglican Church placed too much emphasis on the Word, whereas the Catholic Church too much emphasis on the sacraments. He would hasten to add that neither is wrong; they are both as important as each other, but it meant that congregations were not equipped to form a balanced view. He was not using these two issues as a specific criticism of either denomination, but more as an example of how church policy has consequences for grass-roots Christians.

One of his main teaching themes was faith. "Faith is what you believe," he would say. If you believed you would not recover from a particular ailment, for example, then you wouldn't, because this was your faith—what you believed. Faith is for what we believe, and is part of the means by which God imparts His blessings, be they for infant baptism, salvation, healing or whatsoever.

Jim often searched for a tenet of belief in a particular denomination which he could use in his teaching to illustrate absolute belief in a truth where "there was not a doubt in their heart"—see Mark 11:23. One might say he was always searching for "the baby in the bathwater".

He latched on to the Baptists' understanding of faith for conversion—making "a decision for Christ". He would then say that faith for healing is exactly the same as faith for conversion. The trouble was that Baptists could appreciate this but non-Baptists, though they knew what was meant, sometimes found that the journey from mind to heart was hindered by denominational culture.

For more years than I can remember Jim subscribed to the journal *Sentinel*, a Christian Science magazine. He not only read it, but also drew upon certain of their beliefs which, from time to time, he would use as examples of Christian Scientists' absolute faith (belief). An important characteristic of Christian Science is the belief that there are no problems, because problems exist only in the mind. Humanly speaking, you might be very sick, but if you know the truth, they would say, then the sickness does not exist. There is no sin so there is no salvation! Jim's point was that they have a cultural belief that is absolute insofar as not focusing upon the problem, and if only we Anglicans could be the same and say the problem doesn't exist because *Jesus has taken it away*, then we could move on to receive God's blessing.

However, we tend to focus upon the problem, so much so that our prayers are generally problem-centred. We ask God to take our problems away—our sickness, our loneliness, our resentment, our rejection, and our fear. This is when Jim would say we can always learn something from others' spirituality.

Someone unaware of Jim's passion for balance, who knew he was a subscriber to the *Sentinel*, might have been horrified that a clergyman of such standing in the Anglican Church should even consider reading about, let alone teach, any virtues of Christian Science. But it was just another example of not throwing the baby out with the bathwater.

Jim often spoke of his experience in the USA when he visited the Bronx and met with the Wilkerson brothers, one of whom wrote the bestseller, *The Cross and the Switchblade.* He was immensely impressed to learn that their ministry, Teen Challenge, had an incredible success rate with drug-dependent teenagers. Conventional medical/physiological interventions offered a less than 2% success rate, whereas Teen Challenge took these street kids in and had a better than 85% success rate! It was a residential facility where full-time ministry was exercised, reminiscent of that at Golden Grove.

The first thing Teen Challenge did was to teach participants that Jesus had taken all their problems away by His atoning death on the Cross. So, step one, if you like, was to cast the problem, the burden (whatever form it took) upon Jesus—the burden-bearer.

When David Wilkerson visited Australia a working breakfast was arranged (possibly by Jim) and the Press was invited. Wilkerson spoke about Teen Challenge and the incredible success rate it enjoyed in getting kids healed of dependencies. Jim said his heart glowed as he heard this good news again and, more particularly, because this was now being shared with Australians, in Australia, with the media present. He could hardly wait for the impact this would have upon the public's reaction the next morning when the news broke in the press.

The following day he bought several different newspapers, intending to cut out the various articles for future reference. However, as he scanned through the papers, he couldn't find a single article reporting David Wilkerson's visit or the previous day's conference! He had a friend in the media who was an editor with one of Australia's leading newspapers and who had attended the press conference. He contacted him by phone and asked, "Where is the story about Teen Challenge?" "Oh, Jim, you are naïve," came the reply. "The public isn't interested in good news, only bad news."

So Jim learned an important lesson about our culture—we are not attracted by good news, but by bad news, leading him to say, "Is it any wonder the Church has difficulty in preaching the 'good news' of the Bible?" There is no balance in our culture because the media, which controls what we are told is happening in the world, generally focuses on bad news! In other words, it's a negative bias that sells newsprint, and not a balanced presentation from which we can draw intellectual conclusions.

As with everyone on a spiritual pilgrimage, Jim grew in his understanding and knowledge of the healing ministry. This meant that he changed, or amended, his views on particular issues. There were those who knew him in the early days of his ministry who formed opinions of his views which were not necessarily his developed or final understanding of certain matters. One such issue might be that of whether or not to seek the help of doctors when one was sick, or to depend upon God alone.

There were certainly periods in his early ministry where he was absolute in his teaching of depending on God alone, even to the exclusion of the medical resource. However, this changed well before his retirement from the Cathedral, and he taught a more balanced approach. He drew upon the medical resource himself on a number of occasions, saying that, if at first, or even subsequently, there was no improvement after prayer, then medical advice should not only be sought, but also followed (together with prayer).

It is necessary to qualify this statement in order not to misrepresent Jim's intent, since he certainly didn't advocate a quick prayer followed by, "Oh well it wasn't God's will, so I'll go to the doctor." The first way was always the God way. Prayer was to be in the full understanding of what God had provided, and to be drawn upon through repentance and faith. Furthermore, if we were unable to exercise faith for this ourselves for any reason, then we were to seek the elders of the church, as instructed in James 5:14.

During the last ten to fifteen years of his life Jim would go to some pains to try to give a balanced teaching about divine/medical healing. He would state categorically that he was not against doctors and was, in fact, in support of doctors. He would say he always had been, but I doubt that this was the whole truth. He would have liked to have been able to be single-minded, except that his experience, for himself as much as for anyone else, was otherwise. Therefore, when he was teaching about divine healing, and the issue of medical resources came up, he would say that he was not a medical doctor but that he did know something about divine healing. The point I believe he was making was that he was talking about something he knew about, and we shouldn't ask him questions on things he knew little about. At other times he would say, "If you want to know about medical healing, go to a doctor, don't ask me."

From quite early on in his ministry, Jim introduced the idea of cause and effect. He said, for example, that cancer is the effect, and that the cause could be something that had occurred in the life of the afflicted person six to eighteen months before the cancer appeared. More particularly, the cause may have been multi-faceted, and it would be the most recent cause that was the straw that broke the camel's back. Such causes could be identified as stress factors, because stress is able to deplete our immune system and, when this happens, free radical cells can grow. They are called cancer, and usually manifest in our "Achilles Heel"—our weakest point. He got all this from a medical doctor, an American, Dr Carl Simonton, who not only had a successful cancer clinic, but had written an excellent book, *Getting Well Again*.

Jim also drew insights from Professor Hans Selye who wrote a book in which he stated that the major ingredient in stress is resentment, and the major requirement in dealing with resentment is the need to forgive. Jim combined these two particular insights with the Bible's teaching, focusing on Jesus' instruction to forgive.

His training in the Social Sciences motivated him to find a connection between a breakdown in relationships, and wellbeing. If he could do that, it would provide the link between relationships and sickness. Jim wasn't promoting these secular books as replacements to the Bible in any way; it was more that, with his Social Science qualification, he could at least put two and two together, and make four.

During the last few months of his life, when he continued to teach at St. Mary's Waverley, he read a number of books by Dr Frederick Bailes, who was born towards the end of the 19th century. Frederick Bailes expressed the view that the mind matters and, more particularly, that everything starts with the mind—our intellectual thought processes. Because Jim referred to this in his preaching over a period of some weeks, one could easily conclude that he was giving more credence to Frederick Bailes' views than to the Bible. Personally, I did think he went a bit far with this, even though I knew he was doing it to emphasise the influence and significance of the mind.

I became a bit of an apologist for Jim at some of his teaching sessions. Because I was always there, and I guess I must have been a little more approachable, people used to come up to me and ask, "Why did he say so-and-so?" and, "Where does this fit into the Bible?". I would try to explain, and I think I usually succeeded. Some of these questions came from people who did not attend regularly. If they had, and if they had heard the whole presentation, there would have been no need for their questions.

AN ANECDOTE

Jenny and I had gone on a cruise. It was on the QE2 and we considered it inappropriate to broadcast this around the Cathedral and/or Golden Grove. We had told Jim in confidence so he would know why we were away for a couple of weeks, and where we had gone. He had been invited to preach at the Cathedral—this was after he had retired—and we later discovered that he had, from the pulpit, explained why we weren't there and where we had gone (thank you Jim!).

Within a couple of days of his sharing this news, a violent storm blew up. It was so severe that we had to go far out to sea—to minimise the risk, according to the Captain. Even so, we were continually thrown out of bed by the pitching and rolling. Unknown to us at the time, and because Jim had let the cat out of the bag, prayer was made for our safe return, as the storm was reported in the national news.

As has been said, one of Jim's favourite sayings was, "The Bible says", but when we returned from our holiday and learned that Jim had made our trip generally known, he told us what the Bible does not say. He said the Bible does not say, "Thou shalt not covet thy neighbour's cruise."

Testimony – Dr John Saxton

➤◆◆◀

I'm very thankful to God and Canon Jim Glennon that I have been given the opportunity to share with you a little of what God has done in my life in 1998. I will be 72 in November. I committed my life to Jesus when I was 25. I am still in love with the beautiful girl God gave me as my wife 46 years ago. We have five married children and 16 grandchildren. For the past 44 years I have been a medical practitioner. For most of that time I have been a specialist in diagnostic imaging, diagnosing diseases from the relatively minor to those that are life threatening—observing the pain but unable to heal it and identifying with the suffering but unable to offer much comfort in my diagnostic role.

Seven months ago I consulted a colleague and an incurable, progressive disease was diagnosed, with a life expectancy of one year. Had I been in my 30s or 40s a bilateral lung transplant would have been recommended. But I am not in my 30s or 40s. Six months ago a second, unrelated, disease was diagnosed. The removal of a small and apparently innocent lump revealed a very aggressive form of cancer. At the time of these diagnoses I could not climb my stairs at home without stopping for breath, and there was no medical prospect of improvement. However, Jesus has taken us on a remarkable journey during this last year—a journey of discovery and a journey of healing. Painful though it has been at times, it was a journey I wouldn't have missed.

On February this year, on the night after my first diagnosis, Jan and I had a long-standing dinner engagement with two close friends. They heard our news, encouraged us, and then gave us copies of Canon Jim Glennon's books, *Your Healing is Within You* and *How Can I Find Healing?* This was our first evidence that the Holy Spirit had gone before us with perfect timing. These books caused a revolution—no, an explosion—in my thinking and my expectation. Jan and I have always read the Bible together, but now we began to search the Bible for God's promises to us, especially for healing, and we began to take them literally. It became evident that the faith in Jesus by which we were sure of salvation was the same faith by which we could be sure of healing of body, mind and spirit.

However, I had a problem. As a doctor I had been trained to accept nothing that did not stand up to rigorous scientific scrutiny. Salvation by faith was not a problem, as it was in the spiritual realm and could not be tested in this life. But physical healing had been the aim of my life's work.

Treatment could only be accepted if it was scientifically based. Where did faith fit in? I was praying about this apparent conflict when Jesus' words came to mind, "Render to Caesar the things that are Caesar's, and to God the things that are God's". I no longer had a problem. I had the answer. Render to scientific medicine the discipline of science and to God and His Word the discipline of faith. It dawned on me that, up till then, I had not really accepted all that Jesus had said. I had been using my own mind and my medical training as the yardstick rather than the word of God. I realised I had to repent of this, and I did. So Jan and I began to act upon the instructions and promises found in God's word.

Overcoming fear was the first hurdle. As I searched the scriptures, the promise of 2 Timothy 1:7 became personal to me. *"For God hath not given us the spirit of fear; but of power, and of love, and of a sound mind."* (KJV). I dismissed the spirit of fear in Jesus' name and claimed the promise of a sound mind. Within 15 minutes those physical symptoms of fear, which I am sure most of you recognise, had gone, never to return.

Receiving healing was the next hurdle. It was pointed out to us that God Himself had said through James, *"Is any sick among you? let him call for the elders of the church; and let them pray over him, anointing him with oil in the name of the Lord: And the prayer of faith shall save the sick, and the Lord shall raise him up; and if he have committed sins, they shall be forgiven him."* (James 5:14-15). And in Mark 11:22-25 we were shown the prayer of faith. Jesus said, *"Have faith in God,"* Jesus answered. *"I tell you the truth, if anyone says to this mountain, 'Go, throw yourself into the sea,' and does not doubt in his heart but believes that what he says will happen, it will be done for him. Therefore I tell you, whatever you ask for in prayer, believe that you have received it, and it will be yours. And when you stand praying, if you hold anything against anyone, forgive him, so that your Father in heaven may forgive you your sins."* It seemed so outrageously simple, but it was directly from Jesus Himself.

Then our friends, Helen and Alan Ford, encouraged us to come to the Wednesday evening Healing Service here at the Cathedral and to see Canon Glennon. We did see him, and we came away affirming the answer and not the problem. We began to thank God for the permitted difficulty helping us to depend upon Him more. We began to comprehend the nature of faith, believing we have received it and thanking God before we see it happen. We began to watch with thankfulness for the first blade, then the ear and then the full grain in the ear. Through Canon Glennon's booklet on Christian meditation, we began to know just who we are as a son and daughter of God and just what is available to us—nothing less than the Perfection, the fullness of the Kingdom of God. These Wednesday evening services have been life-giving. We have been anointed with oil and we have received the prayer of faith. Alan and Helen Ford taught us to praise God through the hardest times. Susan, and other members of this congregation of brothers and sisters, prayed for us when we doubted, and continued to affirm that "the perfection is within you, you have what you accept, so why ask for what you already have?"

In August, Jan and I attended a cancer weekend at Golden Grove.

After my years in clinical medicine, I felt the weight of illness in those around me to the extent that one of the ministry team noticed and told me to stop it. But I couldn't. By Saturday night I wondered if I should stay. Then on Sunday I received counselling such as I have never received or even seen before. I didn't say a word. But I received from God the Father through one of the ministry team, deliverance and emotional and spiritual healing beyond all that I could ask or imagine. Later, during a time of meditation and laying on of hands, the Lord gave me a vision. I experienced a rush of warmth through my body that made me gasp. Although fully awake I saw that I was in a hospital ward, as a doctor with a senior physician whom I didn't know. He wasn't wearing a stethoscope and I realised that he didn't need one. It was The Senior Physician, Jesus. So I took him on a ward round of all the people at the cancer weekend and handed them over to Him. I knew immediately they were all safe and the weight of their illness was lifted from me.

When I received my first diagnosis in February and was too short of breath to walk up my stairs at home, as an act of faith I bought a bush walking stick and I called it "Faith" to help me appropriate my healing. Ten days ago, Jan I set off in the car, with my stick of faith for five days of solitude. At Shoalhaven Heads we climbed Mount Coolangatta and as we placed one foot in front of the other, climbing higher and higher, we knew that God was doing something wonderful. Two days later we travelled further south to Tilba Tilba near Narooma, where we set out to climb Mount Dromedary. I believe we climbed about 3000 feet in two hours. Much higher than my stairs at home! As we neared the summit, a cloud descended on the mountain and enveloped us in a cool soft mist.

As we stood in the moist stillness in a cathedral of towering eucalypt trunks, we praised our wonderful God and Saviour in the joy of the Holy Spirit. And we will continue to praise Him, come what may, knowing that nothing can separate us from the power of His love in Jesus.

I urge you to open your arms to accept all the blessings that God has for you in Jesus. They are more abundant than you can imagine.

Dr John Saxton, MB BS FRACR

11

Perfection everything

A GLENNONISM

Why ask for what you've got? You have what you accept.

Having spoken about Jim's pre-occupation with seeking balance, there were times when he went completely the other way. The reason for this was, I think, because he wanted people to know what was available, by which he meant what God had provided, and he didn't want to water it down in any way. In other words, he didn't want another "shandy". He had learned that in any presentation, if he spoke about ten issues, nine of which were positive and one negative, there were always those who latched on like limpets to the single negative point above all else.

Jim often spoke about a family who had a daughter born with scoliosis, or what would more commonly be called a "hunch back". The child had a concave chest causing breathing and other respiratory difficulties. The parents were believing Christians. They believed,*"the kingdom of God is within you"* (Luke 17:21), and they also believed they had what they accepted. So they accepted God's perfect healing for their child by planting the Kingdom seed (faith for healing) and believing it would grow. It didn't happen overnight, but it did happen progressively.

When the parents were asked how they prayed, they didn't give the expected answer. They didn't say they knelt, hands together looking heavenward, or that they prayed for two hours every day. Their response was, "Oh, we don't speak out words or anything like that; we simply believed so that it became a way of life. We believed every moment of every minute in everything we said, thought, or did, so that it became the real us." Jim called this "Absolute Perfection":-

Always have in mind that the whole Christian position, including the Healing Ministry, rests on the fact that Jesus Christ has taken all our problems away in His atoning death. The sin of the world, our fallen human nature, our sickness and infirmity, died with Christ, and the Bible says we are to reckon ourselves dead indeed unto that which died with Him on the Cross. It has to be said that the medical profession is built on a false premise; the doctor puts a label on our ailment and prescribes remedies, all of which are man-made, and virtually all have side effects, so the last stage can easily be worse than the first.

The Christian premise, rightly understood, is that God has already moved every mountain and in its place has restored to us the Kingdom, which is Perfection.

The Kingdom lost in the Fall is the Kingdom regained through the death and resurrection of the Lord Jesus Christ. The Kingdom is now, as well as not yet. The last enemy to be destroyed is death, and we have to wait on the second coming of the Lord Jesus Christ to have that blessing, but many other parts of the Kingdom are available now, including all material provision. Jesus said, "But seek ye first the Kingdom of God, and his righteousness; and all these things [all your material needs] shall be added unto you." [8] *Have in mind also that Jesus said the Kingdom was like planting a seed, which grew until it became the biggest of all trees.*

---

8   Matthew 6:33 KJV

For these reasons we should see things as God sees them, which is "complete, lacking in nothing".⁹ This is a big change from our normal way of seeing things, but it is the way God sees them, and it is the way we should see them. In other words, do not react in terms of the problem but react to the problem in terms of the answer and the Kingdom Perfection. See everything and everyone, and at every time and in every place, perfect as God is perfect; perfect, as God has provided it to be for us in our world today. Jesus said, "Be ye therefore perfect, even as your Father which is in heaven is perfect".¹⁰

If you will do this as a way of life, you will find that the heavens open and you experience in blessed reality the perfection of God's Kingdom here and now. Perfect everything. Perfect everything. Perfect everything.

There are few who would argue against these principles. The important thing, however, is in the words, "If you will do this as a way of life."

If we are ever going to get anywhere, we have to get past the point where we say, "But it's not working (yet)." Even if we say to ourselves, "I will be patient and wait for God's blessing" — this is of itself counter-productive. We have to exercise faith so that we think and say and do and accept and believe, "I have been healed!" As with "I have been saved!" "I have been forgiven!"

Jim said he was always trying to make things clear to himself about how to draw upon God's blessings in healing. He had always bemoaned the Church's limited teaching in this regard and was greatly encouraged when, in 1978 the Lambeth Conference, meeting in England, unequivocally endorsed healing of the sick as part of the ministry of the church. He referred to it in a sermon preached at the Cathedral in January 1982. The Bible reading on the day was Exodus 15:22–26.

It is nice to look out on the Cathedral from the pulpit and to see every available seat taken at the Healing Service tonight. I am beginning

---

9   James 1:4 NKJV
10   Matthew 6:48 KJV

a series of three addresses that I have called, "The Great Promises of God", and the promise I am speaking about tonight is described in the book of Exodus in the Old Testament, "I am the LORD who heals you".[11]

Before I come to that, I want to talk for a while about the promises of God. The first requirement, if we are going to have an effective prayer life, is that we must know what God has promised to give. This is what is meant by the words "Old Testament" and "New Testament", one being the old promises and the other being the new promises. We find the promises that God has made in the Bible as a whole, and the New Testament in particular, especially in the teaching of our Lord Jesus Christ.

Then there is a need for us to relate one promise to another. For example, if you were speaking about the promise of healing you would also take into account that the Bible says that the last enemy that shall be destroyed is death. Death has not yet been destroyed so we don't urge healing to the point where it does away with death, for that would be to urge one statement of Scripture at the expense of another. 2 Peter 1:4 sums it up—God has granted us "his very great and precious promises".

There is something more about the promises of God that I would like to share with you and it is this. It says in 2 Corinthians 1:20 that all the promises of God find their Yes and Amen in Him. That means that the promises of God reveal the will of God. These are things God has promised to do for us. God says, "Yes" to these things. Then it goes on in Ephesians 3 that we are to be partakers of the promises of God. We are to experience them in the reality of our lives.

Summing up what I have said so far: we are to find the broadly-based promises of the Bible and we are to relate one promise to another. They reveal to us the will of God and, for that reason, we are to be partakers of them in our real-life situation. If you make

---

11   Exodus 15:26

this the way you read the Bible you will find that gradually and progressively you will build up a picture of these things in your mind and your heart.

Now I want to refer in particular to the promise of healing, "I am the LORD who heals you", Exodus 15:26. There is much in the Old Testament, or old promises, and there is much more about healing in the New Testament, or new promises. We only have to read a page of our Lord Jesus Christ's life and ministry to know that He made it one of His great themes. It also says in the New Testament that this is what we are to be concerned about as well. People in the Healing Service know well the great text in James 5:14 "Is any among you sick? Let him call the elders of the church…and the prayer offered in faith will make the sick person well." There you have a continuation of this theme of healing as it is outlined for us.

It is a great help to know what the leaders of our Church have said on the promise of healing. I have been greatly encouraged as an Anglican Churchman by the last meeting of the Lambeth Conference in 1978 on the subject of healing. Let me explain if some of you are not sure what the Lambeth Conference is. It is a conference that meets in England approximately every ten years where all the Diocesan Bishops (that is, a Bishop in charge of a Diocese) and Archbishops meet for a month-long meeting under the chairmanship of the Archbishop of Canterbury. They issue, at the end of the Lambeth Conference, an encyclical letter in which they speak to the faithful in the Anglican Church worldwide about their deliberations. Following their last meeting (1978) this is what they said about healing today.

"The Conference praises God for the renewal of the ministry of healing within the Churches in recent times and re-affirms:

1. *That the healing of the sick in His name is as much a part of the proclamation of the Kingdom as the preaching of the good news of Jesus Christ;*
2. *That to neglect this aspect of ministry is to diminish our part in Christ's total redemptive activity;*

3. *That the ministry to the sick should be an essential element in any revision of the liturgy (see the report of the Lambeth Conference of 1958)."*

It is a tremendous encouragement to all the faithful members of the Church to have the leadership of our Church so solidly behind the healing ministry. Of course it is what the Bible says that is important, but it is encouraging that our leaders worldwide interpret the Bible in this way and encourage the members of the Anglican Church to believe the promise of healing.

What we want to say in the long run in talking about the promise of God for healing is that if you have come tonight in need, if you are listening in on FM radio[12] and you have a need, that you can come close to God and believe for His healing blessing. Later in the Service and during the broadcast when we have the laying on of hands, we will be acting this out in practice.

May I add one thing more of a pastoral nature; the only thing that worries me about the Healing Ministry is the person who comes once and then doesn't come again whether they are in the Cathedral or listening in. I want to make the point (and I'll be speaking about this next week in another sense) that we need to draw on the promise of healing with patience. You need to continue to come. You need to continue to listen. I like the words in the Bible that say, line upon line, precept upon precept, here a little there a little. Or the other way it is put when it speaks about the answer coming like the growth of a plant, the blade then the ear then the full head of corn.

If you will keep on with your own faith, and draw upon the guidance and faith of others as well, there is no limit to the good things that God can do for you since He says, "I am the LORD that heals you."

Let us pray: Our loving Father, we praise you that you have made to us precious and very great promises. We praise you that they

---

12   At this time Jim's Healing Ministry sermons were broadcast live over Sydney radio station 2CBA-FM.

find their "Yes" in you and we praise you that we are partakers of them. And we thank you for your promise which says the prayer offered in faith will make the sick person well. We now draw upon those blessings for each one here and each one listening in on the radio, through Jesus Christ our Lord.

AN ANECDOTE

The following event took place in the Cathedral. A particular young lady — I shall call her Samantha — had been blessed with divine healing. Her problem was a urinary tract infection that had persisted for a very long time and was unresponsive to medical treatment. The result was an extremely painful experience every time she took a "wee". Now, Jim was blissfully unaware of this, and also to the fact that Samantha needed to "go" towards the end of the service. As those familiar with the Cathedral will know, the toilets are en route from the Cathedral to the adjacent Chapter House where the congregation gathered after the service for fellowship. Following his usual practice, Jim stood at the exit door between the Cathedral and the Chapter House to greet people and bestow a blessing on them as they passed by. All of a sudden, Samantha raced up the stairs from the toilets in the opposite direction to the flow of people, launched herself at Jim with a hug and a kiss and declared in a loud voice, "I've just had the most wonderful wee." Jim reacted like a stunned mullet, but quickly regained his composure and said, "How nice." Samantha could have said she had just been healed, but her words simply reflected her unique situation — of which Jim was completely unaware!

Testimony – "Maggie"

During our time as leaders of the cancer support ministry Jenny and I were privileged to meet many remarkable people from every walk of life, all of whom carried emotional "baggage" which undoubtedly contributed to their diagnosis of cancer. We heard the most harrowing of life's experiences, and thought we had heard it all—and then along came "Maggie". This is her story.

Maggie walked into the Healing Ministry Centre one Tuesday morning for a counselling session with Jenny and another Healing Ministry elder. As a result, she was invited to the following weekend's residential cancer support group. Initially she refused the offer—"I can't afford it"—but God intended Maggie to be there, and that very morning a $60 donation was received, with the request that it be used to enable a cancer person to attend. This had become the pattern year after year and donations flowed in from people attending these weekends as well as from their families and friends in return for blessings received. We never refused a person who wanted to come, and God always provided exactly the right number of beds for attendees. The fund subsequently swelled to several thousands of dollars and we established the "Samaritan

Fund" for the express purpose of enabling unfinancial people to attend. Many people were able to participate in these healing weekends because of the generosity and love of others; Maggie found herself in a situation where she could not graciously refuse, and so she came.

It was not an easy situation. Jenny was regularly faced with having to uncurl Maggie from a foetal ball, buried under layers of blankets, and having to persuade, cajole and sometimes drag her out of bed to join the others in the group. Lack of self-worth and a deep sense of shame engulfed Maggie whenever left to her own devices, but help was at hand in the form of powerful prayer warriors who spent the entire weekend praying for participants and taking authority over just such situations. Maggie eventually learned that all she had to do was receive God's abundant love.

Gradually, and with help from the Holy Spirit, the barriers Maggie had erected around her life in an attempt to blot out years of sexual abuse and cruelty, came tumbling down. Her life story was so appalling that we marvelled at her courage to go on living, and indeed, in the years that followed she often came perilously close to "throwing in the towel" but always, when deeply challenged, she found the energy to come to the support weekend and learn how to face her demons in a safe environment.

It would be safe to say that Maggie "hung on to every word" Canon Glennon uttered. *"… by his wounds you have been healed."* (1 Peter 2:24) became her personal affirmation. She began to enjoy the company of like-minded Christians and renewed her commitment to God. She became a very popular member of the Healing Ministry, both at Golden Grove and the Cathedral, but then…she started to get sick again. She lost weight, her hair fell out and she had to struggle around on two walking sticks. She had cancer in her bones and liver. Finally, she was admitted to hospital for surgery. But then the doctor had to tell her there was nothing he could do! She was crushed.

She returned to her tiny flat and reached for the bottle of alcohol, the only friend she knew she could rely upon. Despite her best efforts Maggie had remained faithful to the bottle. Through all the counselling and prayer sessions with Canon Glennon and other Spirit-filled warriors, no-one had yet received a "word" that this was the ultimate demon in her life. Even while undergoing chemotherapy she was still drinking, and this caused endless conflict in her spirit.

As she lovingly raised the bottle of elixir which quietened all voices and brought her respite from the reality of her presenting circumstances, she suddenly found she could not swallow a single drop. No matter how hard she tried she couldn't open her mouth. She looked at the bottle and, with a firm voice, declared, "I'd better get serious about Jesus!!"

That was six years ago, and Maggie has not looked back. She put her life on hold for two years. She used an answer machine to filter out negative messages and words; she meditated on the Word of the Lord day and night, going to spiritual retreats, and fasting. She forgave anyone in her life who had ever hurt her, and asked forgiveness from everyone personally, or in prayer, "for her part in the breakdown of their relationship". She soaked herself in the purifying love of Jesus and would not let Him go until He blessed her. Maggie looked for, and expected, healing to be manifested and, as it occurred, she claimed the victory of Christ.

Her faith was, and is, unshakeable as she repeats the words, "Jesus loves me and by His stripes I am whole and complete, reflecting Kingdom Perfection in my Spirit, my Mind and my Body." She radiates health and vitality, and witnesses to the work of the Lord in her life through His good and faithful servant Canon Jim Glennon, whose teaching on Kingdom Perfection and walking on the Kingdom Plane had sunk into the deepest reaches of her consciousness in times of appalling despair and sickness, re-surfacing at her times of felt need.

She remains a true and dedicated friend and a powerful prayer warrior who continually witnesses to others of her Great and Glorious God. Maggie is a living example of what Jim would say is, "believing by faith without so much as putting in a comma or a full stop"—the fundamental teaching of a very great and rare Christian teacher whose words undoubtedly led her to the point where she was ready to acknowledge and accept her total dependence upon Jesus. Yes, she had been brought to the end of her tether—not by God, but so that God could use the circumstances to enable her to depend upon Him more. Jim often quoted the following text written by the Apostle Paul, from his own similar experience. *"We do not want you to be uninformed brothers about the hardships we suffered in the province of Asia. We were under great pressure, far beyond our ability to endure so that we despaired even of life. Indeed, in our hearts we felt the sentence of death. But this happened that we might not rely on ourselves but on God, who raises the dead."* (2 Corinthians 1:8–9).

Canon Jim's final word would have been, Amen, Amen, Amen, Amen, Amen, Amen, Amen.

12

The Great Exchange

A GLENNONISM

We all have faith; faith is what we believe!

From time to time Jim would ask me how I thought things were going, in a ministry sense. I assumed he was seeking assurance that he was getting his message—God's message—across. At such times I took the opportunity to suggest getting back to basics. One such occasion resulted in a presentation he gave at St. Mary's Waverley in about May/June 2003 which he called, "The Great Exchange". The message had to do with exchanging sickness for healing, disharmony for harmony, loneliness for fellowship, and many other problems for their relevant solutions. This might sound a bit unusual, yet, as Christians, we would understand exchanging separation from God with reconciliation, as well as exchanging sin for righteousness, since this underpins our understanding of salvation.

As already mentioned, Jim would say that the gospel means "good news" and would quote Mark 1:14-15, "*... Jesus went into*

Galilee, proclaiming the good news of God. 'The time has come,' he said. 'The kingdom of God is near. Repent and believe the good news!' ". Therefore, Jim said, the "good news" is all about the Kingdom of God.

We need to understand the scriptural basis for "The Great Exchange" in order to know what God has done, so that we react correctly to the circumstances of each unique situation. "I tell you this every week", Jim would say.

The question we should ask ourselves is, what is the Kingdom? There is plenty in the Old Testament about kings. The people wanted a king; they wanted to be ruled, have structure, be provided for, taken care of. They thought that to be reigned over was a benefit, even though there was some confusion in their minds about the difference between an earthly and a heavenly king. The Bible says, *"even though the LORD your God was your king."* (1 Samuel 12:12).

But let's go back a bit further, to the original Kingdom where God ruled over mankind — Adam and Eve. They lived under His reign and in His Kingdom. We are given a picture of their relationship when we are told that the LORD God walked with them in the Garden (Genesis 3:8). We know this as the Garden of Eden, but there is no doubt that it was the Kingdom. Everything was perfect, so we might call it Kingdom Perfection.

Jim would emphasise this at every opportunity — that the Kingdom was lost through one man, in consequence of his disobedience. The Bible tells us what happened, and it is referred to as "The Fall". Mankind was removed from the Garden, and had to toil for food and clothing. Having lost the Kingdom, nothing was perfect any more. Man lost his direct relationship with God, resulting not only in death, but in sickness and infirmity — the effects of what may be termed "corporate sin".

Jim's teaching was that God's plan and purpose, as revealed to us in the Bible, is to *restore* the Kingdom to us — that's the good news! So, as wonderful as salvation is, it is not of itself the good news; it is a means to an end.

In Old Testament times God provided the means for His chosen people, Israel, to have their sins forgiven through repentance and belief. They believed that if they took a lamb of perfect proportions, that is to say, having absolutely no blemish (so there was no justification to otherwise harm the animal), they could *exchange* their sin for forgiveness. As they came in repentance they laid their hands upon the head of the lamb, transferring their sin to the animal. In other words, an exchange took place. The lamb was then slaughtered in front of them so they could see the seriousness of their situation. As the animal died, their sins died with the animal. It was a substitutional atonement for their sins.

It would be correct to call this "an exchange" but, great as it was, it was not, in fact, "The Great Exchange". In the fullness of time, God developed His plan and purpose. There was to be a new way of doing things — *"And so John came, baptising in the desert region and preaching a baptism of repentance for the forgiveness of sins."* (Mark 1:4). When John the Baptist saw Jesus coming towards him he said, *"Look, the Lamb of God, who takes away the sin of the world!"* (John 1:29).

When Christ died, He took three things to Himself, the sins of the world, our fallen human nature, and our sickness and infirmities (because they all came about through corporate sin). *"Therefore,"* the Bible says, *"if anyone is in Christ, he is a new creation; the old has gone, the new has come! All this is from God, who reconciled us to himself through Christ and gave us the ministry of reconciliation: that God was reconciling the world to himself in Christ, not counting men's sins against them."* (2 Corinthians 5:17-19).

We are reconciled to the Father both *now* and for *eternity*. As a consequence of Jesus' substitutional atonement, God has been able to restore the Kingdom to us. Jesus said, *"… the kingdom of God is within you."* (Luke 17:21). There is a *now*, as well as an *eternal*, blessing.

All disharmony and disease resulted from the sin of the world, so God's plan and purpose for Jesus was to deal with this situation, and all its consequences, once and for all. Because Jesus was born of a human mother, and conceived of the Holy Spirit, He became representative of man, and although tempted in as many points as us, yet He was without sin. So, on the altar of the Cross, He was morally perfect. As His blood was poured out, there was a remission of sin (and of all its consequences) for *all* who put their trust in Him. If we put our trust in Christ because of what He did upon the Cross, it is as if we had not sinned. *"Though your sins are like scarlet, they shall be as white as snow;"* (Isaiah 1:18).

What does all this mean? Jim would say, "A full circle has been turned." The Kingdom, lost through one man, Adam, has been restored through one man, Jesus. And the benefit to us? The answer to this question is to be found in the Scriptures where we are told that God has given us, "... *his very great and precious promises*," (2 Peter 1:4). Salvation is one of these; healing is another!

It wasn't uncommon during counselling to have brought someone to the point of *"casting their burden on the Lord"* only to be asked, why on earth would He want it? The answer to this question is fundamental to having an understanding of The Great Exchange which includes, but is not limited to, salvation or even healing for that matter. It's the reason why Jesus came.

As previously mentioned, in the Healing Ministry we have always considered it more important to first meet people at their point of felt need than to try to convert them. Here are the stories of two people who accepted Jesus and believed they were saved. The first—we'll call him George—was a person who, to all intents and purposes, had everything he needed; a relationship, a job, a home and family, good health and harmony. He had always been spiritually aware, and one Easter Friday he went to church and responded to an altar call. He accepted Jesus as his Saviour, thereafter believing himself to be a Christian. There were many invitations to join activities in his church but he was a busy man—the job, the family, etc.—it was as much as he could do to get to church on an occasional Sunday. When he did, he came out feeling "really good", and considered everything was going according to God's plan. Things other than the church controlled the structure of his life, but at the back of his mind he believed he was okay because he had been "converted".

The second person—we'll call her Stephanie—had a very different lifestyle. She had no relationship and no job; she never felt really well, and her whole adult life seemed to reflect disharmony. Stephanie couldn't understand if her depression caused her circumstances or if her circumsances caused her depression. Fear had set in and her fears were all coming true. *"What I feared has come upon me, what I dreaded has happened to me"* (Job 3:25).

A friend suggested to Stephanie that she might like to go to a Healing Ministry service. Her response was that she didn't need healing—she wasn't actually sick—so she refused. Needless to say, she got worse and, a year later, she *was* sick (as well as depressed). In her desperation she called her friend who took her to a Healing Ministry service at St. Andrew's Cathedral.

The elders *first* met her felt need—that is to say, they believed for her healing, laying on hands, and applying the principles of James 5:14. Stephanie had been depressed etc. for nearly ten years, and it took about six months before fear was a distant memory. Her depression lifted and she started to socialise. She began asking questions about Jesus and how it was that she could have been set free from all her burdens. It was at this time the elders led her into salvation, and she accepted Jesus as her Lord and Saviour.

The Church's first responsibility should be to meet people at their point of felt need so that the person receiving pastoral care, experiences a tangible expression of God's love. Otherwise it can be a great "turn-off" to be rushed into conversion; or (like George) it can be meaningless if he is only taught Jesus is Saviour instead of Stephanie who was taught Jesus is Lord and Saviour.

AN ANECDOTE

Jim was known for his various sayings, one of which was a quotation from Charles Spurgeon who said: "It is as important to know what something is not, as well as what something is." The following anecdote illustrates this.

Byrl (pronounced "Burl", rhyming with "girl") would have been one of the longest attendees of Jim's healing services at the Cathedral, and also went to Golden Grove at least a couple of times a week. At one time she had moved out of her unit and into Golden Grove for a few weeks because she said she had an infestation of rats and had called in the vermin experts to put down baits. She was extremely upset because she was a lady who took great pride in her appearance, and in the cleanliness of her unit, but she had come to the end of her tether.

I was serving on the Board of Directors at this time and also saw to the maintenance at the Centre. The then Centre Manager, June Gilbert, would make up a running list of things needing my attention, and I would do electrical, plumbing and concreting jobs, as well as repairing washing machines etc.

Byrl enjoyed her extended stay at Golden Grove but became nervous when she had to go back home. She would have been in her late 70s at the time and lived alone, her husband having long since gone to be with the Lord.

The night she returned home I had a phone call from Jim who had received a most upsetting call from Byrl. He had been unable to console her, and prayer had not helped either. Because I was Mr Fixit, and lived in the next suburb to Byrl, whereas Jim lived the other side of Sydney, he asked if I could go around to see her. I phoned first. Byrl was in tears and distraught as she explained that the bait had not worked and she could still hear the rats squeaking. I could hear them myself down the phone line. I went straight round, and Byrl collapsed in my arms at the front door, trembling in fear.

After a few moments my ears latched on to the sound. I reached up to the ceiling and unplugged the smoke alarm—the battery was flat and it was sending out its signal to be replaced—"squeak squeak … squeak squeak!"

If Byrl had had a million dollars she would have offered it to me then and there, but I settled for a cup of coffee and a biscuit, while she told me of all she had been through during the last six weeks. Apart from the fear and anxiety caused by "what it was not", she had made so many phone calls for help, including calls to Jim. She said she was too embarrassed to tell him "what it was", so I said I would tell him as soon as I got home. I couldn't see Jim's expression over the phone, but I bet it was a picture! We all had many a laugh over that in subsequent years, and Byrl was able to laugh with us—eventually.

Jim goes flying with Andrew Pitcher in a by-plane at age 55 years

13

Two difficult issues

Jim rarely, if ever, taught on the subject of death, and he had sound reasons for this; it always led to a negative reaction from audiences, which often included those with life-threatening illnesses. People didn't want to hear about death because it was generally considered to be a failure in the healing process.

However, Jim's view was that death is the ultimate healing and, for those who had accepted Jesus as their Lord and Saviour, it was the final journey to wholeness we all take. On the few occasions when he spoke on this subject it was to a limited audience. He never referred to it as something he feared, so why was it that he wouldn't publicly discuss the subject?

It was, as earlier mentioned, because he was very much aware of our propensity to engage in negative thoughts and discussion, particularly when there is little or no understanding of God's healing power. He would relate this to our fallen human nature which would often lead us along the wide road to destruction, because we just couldn't help ourselves.

Jim would often remind us that there are two primal instincts; one is the sex drive, and the other is the will to live, yet both birth and death are out of our control. We are conceived and ultimately delivered into this world from a non-breathing environment—the womb—into a breathing environment. We might say we don't want to experience birth, but we are forced to. At the other end of the human cycle, we depart from this world, again albeit unwillingly, from this breathing environment into another world. We refer to this place as Heaven, a place where God and Jesus dwell surrounded by angels and, it would seem, a multitude of ten thousand times ten thousand souls, and more.

I can recall a seminar at Golden Grove when there were about 80 delegates attending. Jim was speaking on how to draw upon the healing power of God, when someone—a clergyman—asked where death fitted into his teaching. Jim replied that he was talking about healing and not about death, but this provoked others to push the point. It soon became clear that the general feeling was that "one died if one was not healed" and so death was a failure. Given that, up to this point, Jim's presentation had lasted an hour, it meant that he had made several references to healing in the Bible, but now the whole focus was upon death as being a failed promise. During the coffee break everyone was talking about death, and no-one was talking about the most valuable points he had taught in respect of healing.

I believe Jim learned that one could easily lose control of a group if a negative issue were allowed into the debate. However good the answer might be, the seed of doubt, fed by our fallen human nature, leads us along the wide road. Jim's solution was, therefore, to teach only about positive issues and not allow questions part-way through a presentation. True it is that death is the ultimate healing, but this is cold comfort to someone who presents with a need for healing. Again, it should be said that the healing ministry is all about meeting people at their point of felt need, and if this is physical healing, then one doesn't talk about death.

Irrespective of whether we have an illness or not, every day we live brings us closer to the day we shall die. Death is the last battle that is won for us through the Passion of Christ and His substitutional atonement by which death loses its sting.

Another subject Jim rarely spoke about was "deliverance". It was not generally known that he was the Archbishop's official representative in deliverance ministry. Any such cases were quietly referred to him, with no publicity or fuss. Jim didn't consider deliverance to be any different to any other kind of healing. His style was quiet but authoritative. There was no screaming or shouting, or any other behaviour sometimes associated with deliverance ministries.

Jim would say that he dealt with such cases by exercising the same authority as he did with any other problem, and by applying the same scriptural requirements — repentance and faith! Following discussion with the person, in order to discover how to pray appropriately, he would cast the burden, or the spirit of infirmity — whatever it might be — upon Jesus and, in its place, accept God's perfect provision — healing — for that person. This would be *his* faith; he would be standing in for the person's need, in believing prayer.

Once, at the Cathedral, when someone was trying to draw attention to himself by writhing on the floor, some members of the congregation suggested that an ambulance be called. Employing Jim's teaching, I took authority in Jesus' name and quietly addressed the person's need in believing prayer.

On another occasion, soon after the terrorism scare, there was a man walking around the aisles during the sermon, saying he was going to destroy the Cathedral. He carried a package which was supposed to be a bomb. There was instant discernment that the man was a "fruitcake", and it was again necessary to simply and quietly take authority in Jesus' name. He was gently encouraged towards the exit, and was never seen again.

Jim would not just leave a person after such ministry. He would pray for him daily, continuing to believe for him in an ongoing way. This would include personal visits or regular phone contact so that the person was supported spiritually through his circumstances of felt need. This is "Ministry", and is far removed from a prayer offered for someone during a ten minute session after a church service.

It is difficult to make comparisons between a church service (however good) with a residential facility such as is offered at Golden Grove where fellowship is provided 24/7. On the other hand, even those who have experienced the blessing of being in residence can very quickly be cut down to size when they leave the spiritual balm provided by other Christians and return to the "world outside". Thus, ongoing support of the kind which Jim practised, is vital.

AN ANECDOTE

An unhappy story I thought initially — but upon reflection it was the kindest thing to do. Early in our ministry, a lady had asked Jenny and I to visit her husband in hospital, to pray for him. There had been much prayer made on previous occasions and, together with Jim, we attended the patient in his private ward. To our utter amazement, Jim prayed a prayer of release, which is to say not for physical healing! Of course, we took his lead and supported him "in faith" but we were shaken to our foundations. Later, Jim explained that one has to be discerning in matters of prayer, and sometimes, irrespective of the difficulty factor (humanly speaking), one has to respond to the guidance of the Holy Spirit. This person was ready to be taken to the Lord, and a prayer for physical healing would have held him, possibly against his own will, in the earthly realm for a few more weeks. Jim prayed for God's perfect blessing for him, confident in his heart-knowledge that God would take him into Glory. Of course, the wife was upset — an under-statement — but later she understood. She had endured several years of seeing him waste away. He had been in continuous pain, and there needed to be a release for them both, to the glory of God. The prolonged emotional pain had brought them both to the end of their tether.

14

Jim in hospital

Keith and Stephen, Jim's two younger brothers, both died from the congenital disorder of the airways and lungs which all three had inherited. Neither were active Christians, although Jim didn't fail in his responsibility in prayer for them—that they would come to know the risen Lord before they died. He believed for them, and left the outcome to God—that is, he didn't ask God for a sign that He was "doing something".

Keith, the middle brother, had "a heart" for the Aborigines and lived and worked among them. When he died, Jim didn't go to the funeral. He couldn't really say why, except that, over the years, they had grown apart, having nothing in common. However, his absence caused misunderstanding among the Aboriginal Elders, especially since Jim was known to be an Anglican clergyman. It wasn't until some time later that Jim received a photo of Keith's gravestone, and realised he had been given a Christian burial.

Jim did visit his youngest brother, Stephen, on his death bed. He told me, with tears rolling down his cheeks, that, all of a sudden, Stephen sat bolt upright and said in a loud voice, "Jesus is Lord". Then he fell back on the pillow and breathed his last. When Jim had composed himself he remarked, "And nobody can say that without the Ministry of the Holy Spirit." So God had met Stephen at his point of felt need, and, perhaps just as importantly, Jim had been God's instrument in fulfilling His plan and purpose.

Because Jim also suffered from this breathing disorder, it isn't surprising that the death of his brothers weighed heavily upon his mind. I had to often remind myself that Jim was only human; it was all too easy to expect him to rise above these circumstances simply because this is what he taught. It is hard, when the circumstances are staring you in the face, to exercise faith for yourself, or for anyone else with whom you are emotionally involved.

As I have mentioned elsewhere, it was not Jim's position to ignore or deny the medical resource, in spite of what many may have thought, given that he preached divine healing. His position was to work with the medical resource and, though this caused him some mental anguish, he was very grateful for it on more than one occasion.

As in so many other areas of his life, Jim tried to arrive at a balanced view where the healing ministry and medicine were concerned. I'm not sure that even he thought he got it right, as you will see from his own words.

Twice he was hospitalised in a serious condition. The first time was mid-2000, when he collapsed and was admitted to the hospital's emergency ward. Jim spoke of this in a message given at the Cathedral on the occasion of the 40th anniversary of the Healing Ministry. At the time, he was barely able to walk, and even standing long enough to deliver a sermon would have been too much in his condition.

In the ancient church the teacher sat down to teach, so I hope you won't mind if I revert to primitive practice. For twenty years or more I have had what is technically called Chronic Airways Obstruction Disease—difficulty breathing. I have been to the doctor and do whatever he says, consequent to which I have been able to carry on, though with increasing difficulty. The last six months I admit I have not looked after myself in the way that I should, and have taken the line of least resistance. So, instead of doing my necessary exercises, I have put my feet up.

On Monday July 31, 2000, I collapsed in my home and called a doctor friend who said, "You must go to hospital." I was admitted to Prince of Wales Hospital through the Emergency Department and was immediately under the care of the Professor of the Respiratory Unit. The second night I was in hospital I collapsed again, but this time even more seriously, and the Professor told me later he thought my end had come. As a last resort I was put on a life support system whereby they paralyse you and artificially ventilate you. I was on that for eight days and nights, and that, in itself, was a highly traumatic experience. I know I kept saying "My last hour has come."

I would like to express my appreciation for every prayer that was prayed for me. In particular to William Delavaga who comes from St. Mary's Waverley, who visited the hospital every day and was permitted to sit in a corner of the Intensive Care Unit where he believed for me five hours every day at a stretch for eight days. It is one thing to pray once a day, or an hour when you think of it. It is quite another to pray for five hours at a time, day after day. That partakes of prayer and fasting, which Jesus said was necessary to move the bigger mountains. At the end of eight days he was exhausted and could go no further. William said at that time, as he gazed out of the hospital window towards the Blue Mountains, God revealed to him that He had already moved every mountain. William then realised, not so much that his prayer had been misguided, but that God had already fulfilled His perfect blessing for me. There was no further need for William to strive in prayer, and he went home for a well-earned rest. It was at that precise time that I was taken off the ventilator and returned to the Respiratory Ward where I stayed for another twelve days. I was in hospital for a total of three weeks and two days.

My problem, my sickness if you like, is that for the last twenty years I have been saying, "I've got a problem, my sickness."

116

When you are anchored to that, it continues on. We all have faith. Your faith is what you affirm and, if you are affirming your problem, you've got faith for your problem and, because it continues on, it will tend to get worse, and when it gets worse, something else comes in. It's called fear. Fear has torment and fear brings about that which you fear, the Bible says. Ultimately you can rub yourself out and that is what I have been doing.

What is the healing ministry? The healing ministry is reacting to the problem by knowing the answer that God has provided and accepting and believing it as well as acting upon it. That is a different story. I had not done that. No, not really. My faith was my problem because it affirmed my sickness. So that we can appreciate the resource God has provided in the healing ministry, we go to the Cross.

I glory in the Cross of our Lord Jesus Christ, for on the Cross, the New Testament says, Jesus did three things:-

1. *He took to Himself the sin of the world, from which comes salvation;*
2. *Our "old man", our fallen human nature, is crucified with Him, Romans 6:6. The Bible goes on to say, if anyone is in Christ they are a new creation, the old has passed away, the new has come;*
3. *And, not least, Matthew 8:17, "He bore our sickness and our infirmity" which harks back to Isaiah 53.*

For that reason, the New Testament says in another place, by His wounds we are healed—because of what Christ has done on the Cross. When Jesus said, "It is finished", those three things died with Christ. This is what the Cross, the Atonement is all about. Jesus said, it is the Father's good pleasure to give to you the Kingdom. A full circle has been turned! The Kingdom is within you; seek first the Kingdom and its righteousness and all your material needs will be added unto you.

Another simile was that it is like planting a seed and it grew, first the blade then the ear then the full head of corn. Because of what Christ has done God has made precious and very great promises which we draw on by repentance and faith. Jesus came preaching the Gospel of the Kingdom saying, repent and believe the Good News.

The healing ministry means we react to our problem by drawing upon the resource God has provided. We do that in repentance and faith. That's a different story altogether to what I have been doing. So what I learned in my sickness was that I had to apply this for myself in my circumstances, and this is what I am now seeking to do.

There are three things we have to know if we are going to appropriate this for ourselves as well as for anyone else. One, we cast our problem, take what form it may, on the Lord. It died with Christ 2000 years ago. We need to appropriate its demise today, so I must cast my breathing problem on the Lord and reckon it died with Christ. We talk about casting our problem on the Lord and then as a kind of a joke (it is really blasphemy) we say, "I took it back again." Well, more fool you, more fool me. The second thing we have to do is to accept healing by faith. According to your faith be it unto you.

The New Testament says two things about faith in Mark 11 and Hebrews 11, "You believe you have received the answer to your prayer so that you do not doubt in your heart" and "Faith is the substance of things hoped for the evidence of things not seen". So, in everyday language, we are to believe we have received healing so we don't have a doubt and we are to believe it before we see it.

This is what Jim shared after his second serious hospitalisation, a year following his first:-

I am a great one for wanting to summarise things; the best teachers are succinct and brief and to the point. If I had to give the briefest description of the Christian healing ministry I would use words that I believe God gave someone I knew who was very ill with, humanly speaking, a fatal disease. God said to him, "Stop saying how sick you are by sight. Start saying how well you are by faith."

Twelve months ago I was very ill with Chronic Airways Obstruction Disease, and my life was despaired of. I have the kind of lungs that you can have as a result of a lifetime of smoking although I have never smoked. In December 1998, after I had come back from the United States, I said, "I am not going to do that again". I had enjoyed my work there but it was stressful and I just said, "I'm not going to go again." Without realising it, I had "retired". The local rector where I worship [St. Mary's, Waverley] has said to me, "You would be amazed the number of men I bury 18 months after they retire." You can have too much adrenalin, and you can have not enough, and 18 months after I had said that, and believed it, I collapsed in the area where I have a weakness, which is my lung capacity.

Through the expertise of the hospital, that I greatly value, and prayer which was made for me continually in the church, I was, by God's grace, raised up. When I realised that my real trouble was that I had "retired", I "switched on" again and since then I have been making excellent progress.

When I was in the hospital 12 months ago they put a lot of fear into me by saying, "If you get a cold you must go to the doctor at once." At the church where I worship we have an hour of prayer every day, Monday to Friday, with an average attendance of six people. At the meeting on Monday week last, there was someone there who had a heavy cold. By the next night I had the symptoms of a cold. When I woke up on Wednesday morning I couldn't speak. I battled through Wednesday, but having in mind the statement of the hospital, on Thursday I went to my GP. He said, "I would not normally provide antibiotics for someone like this but I will for you." So I was put on this course of antibiotics.

On Thursday and Friday I was all right because I was saying, "How well I am by faith", and my experience is that, if you hold on to that, you come out on top. I was in Christian fellowship, and that's important too.

On the Saturday I normally have a quiet day in my home but I was on my own and the symptom of my trouble was that I was having difficulty in breathing. Because of that, and because I wasn't having the fellowship, I found — in spite of myself, in spite of what I believe, in spite of what I have said — I was beginning to say how sick I am by sight. The more I affirmed my difficulty the worse it became, and the worse it became, the more I affirmed my difficulty, and by the time the evening came I was in a bad way.

119

When I retired for the night I found I couldn't lie down without losing all breath completely so I sat up all night in a chair dosing myself up to the eyeballs with the medication I had. I thought, during the night, I would call an ambulance and get them to take me to the hospital. I stuck it out affirming faith as well as I could but really thinking how sick I am by sight until, by 6.30 on Sunday morning I could endure it no longer, and I called William Delavega who lives not far and had taken me to hospital before at my request. I might say William's first time of prayer every day begins at 4am. He prays till 7.30am so he was in his prayer room when I rang.

He was at my home in a quarter of an hour. He took me to the hospital where I had been an inpatient. The triage sister saw me at Emergency and within two minutes I was being treated with oxygen and steroids, and that immediately relieved my situation immensely. I am a Medicare patient. My experience is that the Medicare patient gets the best. They informed the Professor of the Respiratory Unit and he was there at 10 o'clock on Sunday morning to check me out and, under their skilled supervision, and their kindness, I have been much better over these three days and I was discharged this morning.

Just in passing, the Professor saw me on the second day and he had doctors with him under instruction and, when he came to my situation he said, "Mr Glennon was seriously ill 12 months ago but now he is very, very, very much better." Doctors don't usually say, "very, very, very" they say "satisfactory" or something like that. I have a different attitude now about my sickness. I am not just taking it for granted. I am saying how well I am by faith. I haven't plateaued but I'm getting better all the time.

What I want to say is, as long as I was reacting to my symptoms by saying, "How well I am by faith", I got no worse. Had I held on to that, my experience is that I would have come through. But, because of the symptoms, and being on my own so much on the Saturday, discouraged by the symptoms, and troubled by them, I began to say, "How sick I am by sight", and in 24 hours I was on my beam end. You have to persevere in affirming the answer and not the problem because whatever you affirm is what you will have.

AN ANECDOTE

After eight days in intensive care, during his first hospitalisation in mid-2000, Jim said, "The nurses gave me a bath today", adding, with a twinkle in his eye, "It was rather pleasant." He had, in fact, been close to death during this time. The professor who attended him told him afterwards, "Your angels had come for you." Jim reflected on this, and asked me if I thought there was a reason for him having been spared. He wondered if he had fallen short in the teaching he had been giving, or if there was a subject which he had failed to address in his teaching ministry. This gave me the opportunity to challenge him about what I felt was his need to deal with a growing resentment he had towards a particular person. He was able to justify his attitude, and, as he himself so often said, "That was the devil of it [resentment]."

Jim would explain this expression as meaning that it is the work of Satan to get us to resent people for their actions instead of forgiving them. In this specific instance, an area of especial vulnerability, he had allowed himself to justify his criticisms to such an extent that he didn't realise a problem of resentment had developed. If not addressed, it would have meant that, in spite of all the good things he had done, he would have been judged by the one thing he had taught but had not put into practice.

We discussed this, and he admitted that he may well have been given more time on this earth because of his need to forgive the person with whom he had been at loggerheads. It came as quite a shock to him to realise this. We prayed together, and I never again heard him utter a criticism of this person.

15

Hobbies and interests

A GLENNONISM

Once you know what to do, do it!

As a boy Jim joined the Boy Scouts. It was after his scouting days, and before enlisting in the Army, that he took drama lessons. Why he did this isn't known. One can only surmise that he might have been trying to address his problem of insecurity, or perhaps it was a way of meeting others in his own age group. He no more wanted to become an actor than he had wanted to become a cleric. In fact, at that time of his life, he didn't know what he wanted to do.

Whatever the reason, he later said that training in acting helped him tremendously when he had to engage an audience, i.e. a congregation. He certainly developed the ability to control a group, large or small, with a mere gesture of the hand or with a lengthy silence. A prolonged gaze around the Cathedral would have everyone on the edge of their seats in anticipation of what he was about to say.

Jim had great admiration for people, past and present, whom he considered to be outstanding leaders. He would often talk of his respect for Sir Winston Churchill, for example, and could recall the great man's various amusing or profound sayings.

At one of our cancer weekends when Jim was teaching, gloom seemed to have descended on the group. Jim digressed from his message to tell a story about Winston Churchill. The story goes that Winston was at a party at the home of Lady Bonham-Carter. It was generally known that he liked a whisky—or four—and, on this occasion, Lady Bonham-Carter approached him saying, "Winston you're drunk", to which he immediately replied, "And you, madam, are ugly; and in the morning, I shall be sober." The laughter that followed Jim's recounting of this little episode lightened the mood in the room, and he continued his teaching.

On another occasion he told of a speech given by Churchill when he had returned to his old school in Harrow. There was a hush as the great man took the podium and the boys were agog, waiting for his words of wisdom. Churchill stood and looked around at the boys and said, "Never give up, never give up, never give up.", then sat down. Jim loved that speech—so brief, so profound, so memorable.

Jim's study of Churchill's life was a hobby which afforded him great pleasure. He knew of Winston's various interests, which included bricklaying as well as gardening, painting and writing. He had many of Churchill's books in his personal library.

The Churchills lived at their property, Chartwell House, for 40 years. Winston made many changes to the property. Unfortunately, his failure to deal successfully with anything of a financial nature ultimately brought the family to ruin and the property was taken over by the National Trust. How could it be, Jim wondered, that someone so incapable of running a household could so successfully bring a country through the Second World War? In many ways Jim felt himself to be a failure too, and yet he was to become so successful in ministry.

Churchill's complexity probably mirrored Jim's own, even though they were entirely different people. As had Jim, Winston suffered from depression—more recent biographical material indicating this to have been a very serious illness which remained untreated in his time of need.

Jim also greatly admired Nelson Mandela, not least for his ability to forgive those responsible for imprisoning him, and for the way he led South Africa through a bloodless transition from apartheid.

Another man for whom Jim had great respect was Field Marshal Montgomery. In fact, on a number of occasions long after the War he communicated with Monty's son David, the 2nd Viscount Montgomery of Alamein, Churchill, Mandela and Monty—all were men of distinction who achieved greatness through adversity.

One prominent man to whom Jim wrote was Australian Governor-General Dr Peter Hollingworth. It will be remembered that Dr Hollingworth's appointment as Governor-General was unusual, as these appointments are usually made from those with a military or political background. Peter Hollingworth, however, was an Anglican Archbishop. He became the target of adverse media attention because of his alleged failure, when Archbishop of Brisbane, to deal properly with a case of sexual abuse by a subordinate cleric. The issue became political, and the media had a field day.

The political pressure on the Governor-General to resign was intense, and when things were as bad as anyone could possibly imagine, Jim wrote him a letter of support which Dr Hollingworth most graciously acknowledged. It was as if there was nobody else in the world who could reach out (I'm sure this was not entirely true) but it didn't matter—Jim did reach out. This is what he was like. He wouldn't follow the flow, especially if it was negative. Perhaps writing letters might not be considered a hobby, but I suggest that a hobby is something one does in happy pursuit of leisure—doing something other than what one was trained for in a career sense.

Although Jim had two books to his name he said, "I am a speaker, not a writer." The decision to write his books was not initially his. In fact, I would go so far as to say that he could never have written a book. He taught and preached without notes. One could hear him present a particular subject and hear him ten years later, and the message would be almost word for word the same.

In about 1973 he was approached by Christian writers Esma and Macarthur (Mac) Job who wanted to make his teaching available to a wider public. Jim had himself begun to entertain the idea of publishing some of his teaching material—but he would never have got round to doing it—hence, the Job's offer came at an opportune time.

In 1974 the Rev. Brian Thewlis, then of St. Paul's Anglican church in Melbourne, transcribed Jim's teaching from cassettes into hard copy. From this, Esma and Mac put the material into book form. *Your Healing Is Within You* was published by Hodder and Stoughton in 1978. More than 150,000 copies were sold.

His second book, *How Can I Find Healing*, was published by Hodder in 1984. Both books were subsequently reprinted in the USA by Bridge Logos, and there have been eight reprints since.

Jim made no amendments or corrections to the reprinted books, and it is testimony to his teaching that there have been no written criticisms of either book by theologians or lay people.

If someone were to ask the man in the street about his hobbies, one might get a response such as, "I've no time for hobbies, not with a family and a job, not to mention a wife", or they may say, "TV", or "Reading". How about "Heraldry and Genealogy"? That's the response you would have got from Jim. The two are inter-related and Jim had a passion for them that was second only to his passion for the Gospel.

Heraldry doesn't only involve Kings and Queens, and Lords of the Manor, but knights of recognition, that is, those who didn't inherit their knighthoods but who were trained for the role of a knight. Puttock's Dictionary of Heraldry explains this: "A Knight—a title of honour derived from the Anglo-Saxon age. Originally referred to those who attended Kings upon horse back as can be seen by their name in any other language. A boy who was destined to become a Knight was generally placed in a household at age of about six years. He spent the early part of his life with the women folk, learning simple household duties. Soon he was given a pony on which he learnt to ride and generally how to look after it. Later he became a Page and waited upon his Lord at table, looked after his armour and weapons and generally learnt to be useful. At this time too, much of his time was spent in learning how to use his various weapons and in familiarising himself with the laws of chivalry. The next step was to make him an Esquire when he would ride forth with his master acting as a mixture between body servant and aide-de-camp. When he was about 18, providing his master thought he was fit in every respect he was Knighted as a Knight Bachelor, the lowest form of Knighthood. From then onwards he would ride into battle with a pennon on his lance, in command of a number of men. There are various orders of Knighthood including the Order of the Garter, the Order of the Thistle, Order of St. Patrick, Order of the Bath, Order of St. Michael, and St. George and Order of the British Empire."[13]

Anyone can claim a Coat of Arms *if* they are able to prove they are of English, Irish, Scottish or Welsh descent, and can prove their male descent, father to son, from someone whose Coat is officially recorded at the College of Arms in London.

In some ways, heraldry is like theology—one never stops learning about it—and Jim was no different to anyone else in this regard. There is a dictionary of heraldic terms, signs and characters which he found fascinating.

Coats of Arms came into being around the period AD 1130–1160, coinciding with the development of sophisticated and virtually total body armour. Since the person under the armour, which included a helmet, was unrecognisable, he wore a coat to signify whose side he was on. Hence the term "Coat of Arms" which, later, was reproduced on shields, flags and caparisons—equipment for horses. Later still, these identifiers were taken up by family groups and clans. Nowadays, the practice has been adopted by sporting bodies. Football teams, for example, and jockeys, wear "colours"; businesses and corporations display "logos."

Jim designed his own Coat of Arms. To do this he had to apply to the College of Arms for Letters Patent, which attracted a fee. Heraldry experts are like solicitors, having their own practices, their own jargon or language; they follow very strict guidelines regarding symbols, shapes and colours in their research of geographic as well as family origins.

Jim was granted Letters Patent by the College in 1985. His design includes the Cross of St. Andrew and God's healing hands—representing his involvement in the Cathedral's Healing Ministry. Two quills represent a scribe, and relate to his two books. At the top are two angels with hands supporting a mountain—which Jesus spoke of in Mark 11:23.

The following inscription accompanies the Letters Patent

---

13   *A Dictionary of heraldry and related subjects* by Colonel A G Puttock published by Blaketon Hall Ltd Exeter ISBN 0 907854 93 1.

along with the coloured Glennon Coat of Arms. The original is handwritten in calligraphy on a pigskin scroll.

TO ALL AND SINGULAR to whom these presents shall come, Sir Alexander Colin Cole, Knight Commander of the Royal Victorian Order, upon whom has been conferred the Territorial Decoration, Garter Principal King of Arms, Sir Anthony Richard Wagner, Knight Commander of the Most Honourable Order of the Bath, Knight Commander of the Royal Victorian Order, Clarenceaux King of Arms, and John Philip Brooke-Little, Esquire, Commander of the Royal Victorian Order Norroy and Ulster King of Arms, Send Greeting! WHEREAS Alfred James Glennon of Boundary Street, Clovelly in the State of New South Wales in Australia, Clerk in Holy Orders, Licentiate of Theology of the Australian College of Theology, Canon of St Andrew's Cathedral, Sydney, Australia hath represented unto The Most Noble Miles Francis Stapelton, Duke of Norfolk, Knight of the Most Noble Order of the Garter, Companion of the Most Honourable Order of the Bath, Commander of the Most Excellent Order of the British Empire, upon whom has been conferred the decoration of the Military Cross, Earl Marshal, that he is desirous of having Armorial Bearings for Glennon granted and assigned under lawful authority and recorded in Her Majesty's College of Arms and hath requested the favour of His Grace's Warrant for Our granting and assigning such Arms and Crest as We deem suitable to be borne and used by him and by his descendants with due and proper difference and according to the Law of Arms, and forasmuch as the said Earl Marshal did by Warrant under his hand and Seal bearing date the Twentieth day of December 1985 authorize and direct Us to grant and assign such Arms and Crest accordingly, Know ye therefore that We the said Garter, Clarenceaux and Norroy and Ulster in pursuance of His Grace's Warrant and by virtue of the Letters Patent of Our several offices granted by the Queen's Most Excellent Majesty to each of Us respectively do by these Presents grant and assign unto the said Alfred James Glennon the Arms following that is to say Argent on a Saltire Gules in chief two Quills the pens inwards Or and issuing in base

Two Hands Proper And for the Crest upon a Helm with a wreath Argent and Gules two Angels kneeling Proper vested Gules winged Or supporting between them a mountain Proper Mantled Gules doubled Argent as are in the margin hereof more clearly depicted to be borne and used forever hereafter by the said ALFRED JAMES GLENNON and by his descendants with due and proper difference and according to the Laws of Arms In witness thereof We the said Garter, Clarenceaux and Norroy and Ulster have to these Presents subscribed Our names and affixed the Seals of Our several offices this Ninth day of January in the Thirty-third year of the reign of Our Sovereign Lady Elizabeth the Second by the Grace of God Queen of Australia and Her other Realms and Territories, Head of the Commonwealth, Being in the Quincentennial Year of the Incorporation by Royal Charter of King Richard the Third of His Kings of Arms, Her aids and Pursuivants of Arms on the Second day of March One Thousand Four Hundred and Eighty Four and in the Year of Our Lord One Thousand Nine Hundred and Eighty Five.

Below the foregoing text, affixed to the pigskin parchment, hang the official Seals of Clarenceaux, Norroy and Ulster.

Jim was proud of his Coat of Arms, which hung on his study wall. The Coat of Arms becomes an inheritance which can be passed on to any male Glennon and, although Jim didn't marry and have children of his own, he does have a cousin who has male offspring. Having established the Letters Patent, a male descendant can claim this Coat of Arms, subject to a registered addition reflecting his own particular family. Naturally, this has to be recorded with the appropriate College of Arms in England.

Jim was made a Member of the Order of Australia (AM) by the Governor-General, Sir Ninian Stephen, in the 1987 Australia Day Honours. This was in recognition of his services to the community and to religion, particularly at St. Andrew's Cathedral. I believe (although he never said so) that he was proud of his accomplishments in the Anglican Church, as well as of the recognition he had earned in every denomination that received his teaching. I think this was more of a retrospective pride, since he certainly could not have felt this way when first employed at the Cathedral, or even in subsequent years. I just feel that, in his autumn years, he reflected upon the experiences that had brought him to where he was, so that towards the end of his term of office at the Cathedral these reflections warmed the cockles of his heart.

AN ANECDOTE

As I have said, Jim admired many well-known people, some of whom he knew personally. However, he never thought of himself as a celebrity, as the following story illustrates. When he spoke of his experiences at drama school, when he would have been in his early twenties, he mentioned the Australian actress, Ruth Cracknell. They were in the same group, and he would tell us about their experiences on the amateur stage. Ruth went on to become a well-known professional actress of stage and television. When Jim told the story he would finish by saying, "… and Ruth went on to become famous"—as if he hadn't! It never occurred to him that, in his chosen profession, he had also achieved fame. This was, of course, because he always gave the glory to God.

Left
*Jenny, Sid and
Canon Jim
farewelling USA
guests after lunch at
Doyles Restaurant,
Watson's Bay*

Right
*Canon Jim Glennon AM
with his brother Stephen
and his wife Joan,
having received his
Australian Merit Award
in January 1987*

130

Canon Jim's self designed Coat of Arms

16

The Canon Jim Glennon
Healing Ministry Trust

A GLENNONISM

And stop belly-aching about your problem.

From time to time Jim spoke to me about his will, and the disposal of his various assets. He didn't have any living relatives, apart from a cousin in Melbourne, to whom he could make any bequests. I am sure that others had similar discussions with Jim, and so, about four years before he went to Glory, he decided to set up a Trust Fund.

The Trust was to provide for the capital to be held in trust, earning interest and dividends, as well as growth, which would be distributed to the various ministries of his choice. Having decided to do this, he felt that others might like to make contributions, which meant that the structure of the Fund had to allow for this.

The next step was to set up a Board of Trustees. Jim's aim was to further the Kingdom through ministry initiatives. There would be no point in having a Board which simply distributed the money to service debt.

He chose certain organisations to be the beneficiaries of the Trust and decided upon a mixture of trustees, representative of these organisations, selected on the basis of the office they held.

The office-bearers, or ex officios, were to be: the Dean of the Cathedral (Chairman); the Treasurer of the Healing Ministry at the Cathedral; the Leader of the Healing Ministry at the Cathedral; the Treasurer and Secretary of the Healing Ministry Centre and the Leader of the Healing Ministry Centre (the same officer as the Leader of the Healing Ministry at the Cathedral). There was also to be a Financial Planning Adviser who was employed by the Glebe Financial Services Group to direct present and future investment strategies. The choice of the Glebe Financial Services Group was in order to exercise an ethical standard of investment as well as ensuring a Christian approach to financial matters. Consequently, there were to be no investments in gambling, tobacco or any other portfolio considered to be outside this ethical standard.

As long as the ex officios held office they were trustees of the Fund. When they left office for any reason the new office bearer would be invited to take up the responsibility as trustee.

Provision was made for three trustees who were not office-bearers, in order to provide balance as well as "non-church experience" to the group. Their tenure of office was to be unrestricted and they could be re-elected annually. These, in particular, were to bring their first-hand experience of Jim's intention to the Trust, whereas any subsequent ex officio holders would have only the written text of the Trust Fund to which to refer.

The Deed of Trust provided for the Healing Ministry at the Cathedral, the Healing Ministry Centre Golden Grove Ltd, and the general ministry at the Cathedral to receive equal distributions of 30%. The work of the Order of St. Luke (Australia), the Bush Church Aid Society (BCA) of Australia, and the Church Missionary Society (CMS) Australia, were to be supported from the remaining 10%. Also included in this last amount is any other work in Australia which demonstrates the principles and philosophy of the Christian ministry of healing, whether these be in churches,

134

theological colleges, healing homes or in the provision of training opportunities.

By virtue of its declared objectives the Trust is a charity and so is protected from the various taxes that would otherwise impinge upon any earnings. It also protects capital investments within the Trust from Capital Gains Tax.

A letter Jim wrote to the Trustees when he was on the Board of Trustees as the Trust Settlor[14] clearly sets out his wishes regarding the Fund.

> *I would personally like to see that the Healing Ministry and the Cathedral both indicate in advance of the money being distributed the purpose for which they would use the money. It would sicken me to think that either the Healing Ministry or the Cathedral or both could anticipate receiving what ultimately will be a substantial amount that would be used only to support their general finances and excuse them from raising their own finances and meeting their own needs. I suppose, in other words, it means that I think the Trust money should be used for fresh endeavour and be a spur and not a crutch.*

AN ANECDOTE

Jim used his wealth to bless other people, but on one occasion Jenny suggested that, for a change, he should buy something for himself. "What do you suggest?" he asked. Jenny thought it would be nice if he bought himself a new car—so he did, a sporty little red Peugeot 306 XT. His long-suffering secretary-in-retirement, Dorothy Bird, made comment about its quality and probable longevity because it was a "thoroughbred" and said, "That should see you out, Canon"—and it did! The car had lasted ten years without a fault, and Dorothy, for sentimental reasons, decided to buy it from the Executors of Jim's estate.

---

14   The settlor's function is to give the assets to the trustee to hold for the benefit of the trust's beneficiaries on the terms and conditions set out in the trust deed. The settlor executes the trust deed and then, generally, has no further involvement in the trust.

17

The Final inheritance

A GLENNONISM

When the mountain is big, faith is often small,
so the mountain gets cast into the sea, spadeful by spadeful.

After Jim's retirement from the Cathedral, and towards the end of his travels, he needed a parish to belong to. One Easter Day he went to the service at St. Mary's Waverley, an eastern suburb of Sydney. Not long after that, the Rector, Fr Terence Dicks, and the Wardens of St. Mary's, approached him about the possibility of establishing a healing service and teaching ministry in the parish. Jim accepted, and an ecumenical group formed the nucleus of a healing service congregation which quickly grew to between 40 and 50 people a week.

St. Mary's shared with Jim the understanding of the whole gospel, and Jim's involvement quickly included the 10am Eucharist as well as individual ministry, counselling and prayer.

Terence embraced Jim's emphasis on the need for prayer. Prayer meetings were started, taking place every weekday except on

Thursdays, which was the day for the Healing Service. The meetings lasted for an hour. They were not specifically for healing, but more to encourage those who attended to reach out to the wider community, and to intercede for the needs of the world.

With every other healing ministry which Jim had planted he had moved back, either to the Cathedral, or to retirement activities. In this situation, however, he stayed, taking up the role of "honorary priest", and was invited to preach as well as to participate in traditional Anglo-Catholic ceremonial processionals. He came to embrace these high church traditions in a most respectful way. Terence encouraged his involvement in the St. Mary's style of worship, so that he felt more and more at home. It was quite amazing that, in his autumn years, Jim should have changed like this, and yet held to his core doctrinal beliefs.

In addition to the Thursday morning teaching and healing service, Jim conducted an evening healing service once a month, and his influence on the parish, in the area of prayer, increased. Terence has said that Jim's influence was significant, both for him, and the congregation at St. Mary's, because his teaching and prayer ministry was so profound, so meaningful, so effective, so Biblical!

Terence and Jim shared a non-judgmental approach in many areas. They accepted people "where they were at", irrespective of their lifestyle. They did this in Christian love, which is not to say they always approved of the lifestyle, or the person's chosen doctrine, but they accepted them.

I clearly remember talking to Terence about one of my own grandchildren. The parents had been refused baptism for their baby at a certain Anglican church. The minister had asked the parents which church they attended, and they truthfully replied that they didn't attend church but felt drawn to seek the sacrament for their baby. They were sent away, being told that there was no point in the child being baptised because of their lack of regular church attendance! I asked Terence the reason for this rejection, and enquired what he would do in such circumstances. He didn't criticise the minister concerned, but said that he, himself, would never refuse to baptise any child, irrespective of the parents' declared belief or perceived doctrine, adding that it was a golden opportunity to minister to the parents in Jesus' name. I asked him how he could take this position. His reply was that if he refused to baptise such a child, on his day of judgment he would have no answer to God's question, "Why did you not baptise this child, Terence?" Jim supported this position, saying he should exercise every opportunity to extend the Kingdom, not only for the child but also for the parents. And so my grandchild was baptised at St. Mary's by Fr Terence.

There was to be much more to the relationship between Jim and Terence than could have possibly been anticipated. In 2003 Terence and his wife Jan were able to get away for a few days up to Queensland for a holiday. This was a pretty rare occurrence, since like all parents (quite apart from parish duties) they were extremely busy. One day, while at the beach, Jan was sitting on a beach chair reading, and Terence had gone for a swim. This was more of a dip than a swim since Terence was not what one might call a swimmer. What happened next is not entirely clear, except that the consequences were devastating.

Jan happened to look up from her book and saw what she thought was a log floating in the water. She looked for Terence but couldn't see him. Then she saw people running down to the water's edge and others dragging Terence, unconscious, from the surf. It seemed he had been "dumped" by a wave; his spinal cord had been seriously injured and he was flown by helicopter to hospital.

There followed several months of anguish for the whole family. Terence was paralysed and unable to move. The medicos had performed a tracheotomy, opening up his throat to enable him to breathe. It was quite a few months before he could be relocated to a Sydney hospital, enabling people other than his immediate family to visit him.

Terence spent almost two years in hospital before going into rehabilitation. It was hard work to regain even the slightest movement of limbs. Ultimately, he was discharged in a wheelchair, and learned to cope. Throughout it all, with the help of God, he displayed incredible courage and spiritual strength. He returned to work as Rector in his wheelchair.

During all this time Jim stood in faith for him, as well as helping him to fulfil his ministerial duties. As Jim would so often say, healing can be progressive, during which time we, at our human level, have much to learn. Up until the time Jim went to be with the Lord he believed for Terence—and, for those who have witnessed the progress of Terence's healing, it has been an ongoing miracle.

After Terence retired, he and Jim maintained a close relationship. Terence attends St. Mary's every week. He ministers to others, and prays for others, as well as operating a phone ministry. Ongoing prayer, in the form of praise and thanks— *"being watchful in the same with thanksgiving"* (Colossians 4:2)—is offered for him every week at the healing service.

Jim's admiration for Terence knew no bounds, and he always spoke in glowing terms of his courage and perseverance. For his part, Terence took comfort from Jim in everything he said and did. When Jim was alive, they stood spiritually tall together in mutual respect and Christian brotherhood. To say that Jim influenced Terence and his ministry would be a gross understatement; everyone could see the bond of respect that existed between them.

Jim not only planted healing ministries, but also maintained ongoing relationships with them. One might say he planted and watered the seed, watching it grow. This applied, not only in the Anglican Church, but in the wider church community—the Body of Christ. He would always step outside his own discipline to bring full gospel teaching to anyone who would listen. He held to his own doctrine, but would accept invitations from any denomination that was open to learn how to claim God's healing power—leading to wholeness and, of course, salvation—which meant that the Kingdom was extended.

I spoke earlier of Jim's material legacy in the form of the Trust Fund which will continue to support ministry initiatives for the express purpose of extending the Kingdom. However, his spiritual legacy includes his teaching on prayer[15]—not just for healing but also for *"Whatever you ask for"* (Mark 11:24), standing in faith for others for healing, salvation, forgiveness, baptism and so on.

The most common observation people made about Jim's ministry had to do with their appreciation of being taught how to pray in the unique way in which he did. He was a teacher who demonstrated his message in front of an audience. One might say it takes

---

15   See Part Two: The Three Main Themes in the Healing Ministry.

courage to stand in front of a group of strangers, invite people to come forward and receive laying on of hands in prayer and expect the prayer to be answered in the present tense, but Jim would have said it's simply a matter of obedience. He would put prayer into practice. But he never thought of there being any merit on his part, since it was not *his* courage any more than it was *his* power. He only ever gave God the credit.

He would say there was no point in praying—however strong our faith—if we then sat on our hands and waited for God to perform. This is where he would quote the Bible saying, *"Show me your faith without deeds, and I will show you my faith by what I do"* (James 2:18) or *"...faith without deeds is dead."* (James 2:26).

Jim taught us how to pray so we could draw upon healing for any situation, irrespective of the difficulty factor. In fact, he would say the greater the difficulty factor, the more this moved him to depend upon God. So he kept telling us what God has provided through the substitutional atoning death of Jesus, as well as how to claim it, so that it became reality. Jesus said, *"...anyone who has faith in me will do what I have been doing..."* (John 14:12).

AN ANECDOTE

I remember an occasion at Golden Grove during a residential cancer weekend when, apart from others, there was a lovely Christian couple attending. They were farmers. The husband had cancer in his bones which affected his hips, making sitting, and walking, painful. His condition was a major drawback in the effective operation of their property. I said they were Christians but, although they went to church regularly, they had absolutely no idea what God was able to do if they were prepared to follow Jim's teaching. So it was, that when Jim invited anyone with a need for healing to come forward, this man didn't come! It was through his wife's encouragement that he eventually struggled out of his seat. In true Anglican fashion he was sitting at the back of the meeting, so he had further to walk, and in pain!

The farmer had no expectation for healing. His wife looked on, hoping for the best but fearing the worst. This didn't matter, because Jim, depending on Christ's righteousness, stood in faith for them both. He prayed the prayer of faith, casting the burden of sickness upon Jesus, and, in its place, accepting God's perfect provision for healing. There was more to the prayer than that but I'm not seeking to transcribe the prayer — it's the principles which are important.

After the prayer Jim asked the man how he was. The reply was that he felt no different. Jim said, reinforcing the message that he was believing for the man, "This isn't done with our feelings; we have to trust in the promises of God." Then he asked the man to do something he couldn't do too well before. He told him to get up and walk to the end of the auditorium — about 20 metres. The guy immediately got up and walked back to his seat, but before he could sit down Jim said, "Now run back here." Without pausing to think, the farmer turned and ran back the length of the auditorium. Okay, he wasn't doing a ten second dash but neither was he walking slowly, in agony! His wife was now on her feet praising God, and he was even more embarrassed than he had been before he first went forward.

We used to maintain contact with many of those who attended these weekends and this couple went on and on, not only healed but in a closer relationship with God. Praise the Lord!

MESSAGE FROM

HIS EXCELLENCY AIR MARSHAL SIR JAMES ROWLAND,

A.C., K.B.E., D.F.C., A.F.C.,

GOVERNOR OF NEW SOUTH WALES

TO THE REVEREND CANON ALFRED JAMES GLENNON, A.M.

ON THE OCCASION OF HIS RETIREMENT

29TH JUNE, 1988

This evening the Healing Ministry at St. Andrew's Cathedral is to farewell you from its leadership. In addition to those in the congregation, many thousands of people throughout this country, and overseas, would wish to show gratitude for the inspiration and guidance you have given to them since you started the Healing Services in 1960.

You have made a great contribution to religion in New South Wales, particularly as Precentor at St. Andrew's Cathedral and within the Diocese of Sydney. Your many friends will miss you during your absence on mission work in England and America, but I am sure all will look forward to your return to Sydney.

Governor

The Governor General

BISHOPSBOURNE
39 ELDERNELL AVENUE
HAMILTON 4007
QUEENSLAND
AUSTRALIA
TELEPHONE: (07) 268 2706

DIOCESAN REGISTRY
417 ANN STREET
BRISBANE 4000
QUEENSLAND
AUSTRALIA

G.P.O. BOX 421
BRISBANE 4001
TELEPHONE: (07) 839 4766

FROM **THE ARCHBISHOP OF BRISBANE**

3RD JUNE, 1988

Deaconess G. Hall,
Healing Ministry,
St. Andrew's Cathedral,
Sydney Square,
<u>SYDNEY</u>. N.S.W. 2000.

Dear Deaconess Hall,

Thank you for your letter telling me of Canon Glennon's farewell in St. Andrew's Cathedral on Wednesday, June 29th. I have great pleasure in sending this greeting:-

"Canon Jim Glennon and his ministry have been known to me over a long period of years now.

Jim Glennon is an Anglican priest of deep prayer, profound sensitivity, a great encourager. The most significant part of his ministry has been his courageous dedication to the Healing Ministry. I would judge that no other Anglican in his generation has made so significant a contribution to the Healing Ministry. But this ministry has been not only for Anglicans, but many other Christians.

I am glad that June 29th, St. Peter's Day, is a Wednesday, this year. and that we can give thanks on a major holy day in our calendar for the ministry and witness of Canon Jim Glennon. His ministry, like St. Peter's, grew as he responded to the call of our Lord Jesus Christ and exercised the ministry entrusted to him.

May God greatly bless him still."

. . . .

I hope that Wednesday, the 29th is a wonderful day for all of you who will be gathering at Jim Glennon's farewell.

Yours very sincerely,

+ John Grindrod.

The Most Reverend J.B.R. Grindrod
<u>ARCHBISHOP OF BRISBANE AND PRIMATE.</u>

The Archbishop of Brisbane

LAMBETH PALACE, LONDON, SE1 7JU

Message from the Archbishop of Canterbury to
mark the retirement of Canon Jim Glennon of
St Andrew's Cathedral, Sydney, New South Wales

I have happy memories of my visit to St Andrew's Cathedral,
Sydney, not least because it provided me with an opportunity
to meet and speak with Canon Jim Glennon.

For 28 years Canon Glennon has been engaged in the healing
ministry, and there are thousands of people who will be
grateful for what he has brought to them. Jim Glennon has
shown that healing lies at the heart of the Christian gospel,
for true healing is intimately related to wholeness.

In the past years Canon Glennon's ministry has extended for
beyond Australia, and there will be many who at this time,
like myself, will give thanks to God for a unique and
distinctive ministry exercised with quiet compassion.

On this day we shall particularly remember Jim Glennon in
the Chapel at Lambeth Palace and give thanks for all that he
has been, and still is, to so many.

Yours sincerely,

Archbishop of Canterbury

The Reverend Canon A.J. Glennon A.M.

The Archbishop of Canterbury

144

Anglican Church Diocese of Sydney

ST. ANDREW'S HOUSE SYDNEY SQUARE NSW 2000   PO BOX Q190 QUEEN VICTORIA BUILDINGS SYDNEY 2000
TELEPHONE (02) 269 0642   TELEX COFE 24183   CABLES 'ANGLICAN' SYDNEY   AUS. DOC. No. DX 878
. . . FROM THE ARCHBISHOP OF SYDNEY

I have known Canon Jim Glennon since he entered
Moore College as a student on his discharge from the Army. I well
remember his appointment as Precentor of the Cathedral in 1956
and the arrangements which were made for him to engage in the
course for a Diploma in Social Studies at the University of
Sydney. This was no doubt a significant factor in cultivating
his skills, his sense of empathy and his understanding of non-
directional guidance and counselling. Though not foreseen at
the time, it helped to prepare him for the ministry which lay
before him once the Healing Service was established in December,
1960.

This Service which began in the most modest
way with a congregation of (ten) people has grown to such an
extent that it has come to touch hundreds of lives. It has
been maintained and continued to develop over the long period of
21 years. It has opened other doors of ministry for Canon Glennon
throughout Australia and overseas. It is today one of the
outstanding ministries in the Diocese of Sydney.

I have always admired the way in which Canon
Glennon has sought to bring everything to the test of Holy
Scripture and has sought above all to exalt the Lord Jesus as
the mighty ever living Saviour. I send my warmest greetings and
good wishes for God's rich and abundant blessing on Canon Glennon
and his continued ministry.

Archbishop of Sydney.

29th October, 1981.

The Archbishop of Sydney

145

18

Just in time – David's story

A GLENNONISM

*The responsibility of faith lies with the church—
the priesthood of all believers.*

I was ill with cancer and was due to have surgery. I had already had two operations to remove tumours from my lungs, and another tumour had developed in my remaining right lung. My Pastor had given me an audio cassette of a "grumpy" sounding man named Canon Jim Glennon. It was called, *You Don't Have To Have Cancer*. On this tape Jim talked about repentance, forgiveness and faith. It was a very inspiring message; it made a lot of sense in my current and past situation. I managed to get Jim's phone number from a mutual friend, and plucked up the courage to call him (after a fair bit of procrastination!).

I explained my situation to him, hoping that he would give me some inspiring answer or "quick fix" but he was silent, and then bluntly told me that I needed to go to one of his cancer weekends at Golden Grove, said goodbye and hung up the phone! I was a bit put out by his approach, but decided that I must go.

The date of the cancer weekend fell exactly on the weekend before my operation which was scheduled for the following Monday morning. My wife, Ann, and I attended, and I remember the first evening we all sat down together in the chapel. Sid and Jenny Eavis told us that this was the only time we were allowed to talk about our disease. For the rest of the weekend we were going to learn how to receive healing. Each person shared his or her problem and when it came to me I felt the fear rise up within me and I became quite emotional. When this time had finished, Canon Jim approached me, pointed his finger at me and said, "We need to talk."

Ann and I sat down with him and he questioned me about the past eighteen months, and even back into my childhood. It was a very interesting discussion. Jim pointed out many things about the relationship between stress/resentment and sickness, and as the rest of the weekend went on, the "penny" was beginning to drop. I did have the operation on that following Monday, and it went remarkably smoothly, but I knew there was more to God when it came to healing.

As time went by, our friendship with Canon Jim grew. We often thanked God that this remarkable man was our friend — that God had brought him into our lives. He taught me how to have faith, and often how to dig deeper into God when the situation got harder. I often say to my wife, "Canon came along Just In Time". It was like Jesus calming the storm. Things were getting gradually worse, medically speaking, but God brought Canon to us at the right moment (when we were ready to hear), and the storm had begun to calm.

I started attending Canon's regular Thursday healing meeting. Canon would tell inspiring stories, teach on healing and faith, and always challenge. He would often tell the story of a friend of his that was in Calvary Hospital dying of cancer. This man was in a coma before death and Canon spoke to him and said, "Stop saying how sick you are by sight and start saying how well you are by faith." Several weeks later he visited the friend, who was out of the coma, sitting up on the side of his bed, waiting to be discharged. He told Jim, "I heard you through the mist. I heard every word you said, and it's all I have been saying for the past five weeks." However, after he returned home, his wife began telling him it was "terminal". The doctors told him how sick he was by sight, and eventually the man passed away. I remember Canon telling this story with tears in his eyes. He was very committed to you if you came to him with a need and were willing to listen to his advice. He would often relate to you by saying how he "learned through the school of hard knocks", and protest, "They don't teach this in churches and seminaries!"

I wasn't just amazed at his commitment to believe for people, but his commitment to follow them up! Whenever I couldn't make it to a Thursday meeting, Canon would call me and remind me (in his subtle way) of the importance of coming regularly (and on time!!). I quickly learned to call him ahead of time if I couldn't make it to a meeting. There was one week that I couldn't come and also didn't call, and, surprisingly, I didn't receive a call that night, so I rang the following day and left a message on his answering machine. Several days passed and—nothing, so I called again, and again—nothing.

It was a few days later that I got a call from a friend who told me that Canon was ill and in hospital, but due to be discharged in a day or two. I was relaxed at this and planned to visit him the next day. Early the next morning I received a call from another friend who had been informed by the hospital that he might not make it through the day. My wife and I were shocked, and urgently got to the hospital, and found Jim in a coma. We stood by and held him, praying and believing silently, and told him how much we loved him and appreciated him. It was just over an hour or two of us being there that he passed away. I was sad that I didn't get to talk with him, but I know he heard me. He cared so deeply for my family, and I know he took much on himself to believe for me when my health was bad, like no other. As we were all standing there by his hospital bed crying, God reminded me that Canon came into our lives Just In Time, and now I was able to see my friend—Just In Time!

Tributes

Here are two tributes to Jim received after his death. The first was written by Rev. Roger Rich from St. Paul's Anglican Church, Melbourne, where the Healing Service they have there has just celebrated its ten-year milestone. Roger is an unashamed supporter of Canon Jim's teaching and will often start a sermon or teaching session with the words, "I make no apology for sounding like Jim Glennon; in fact, if I do, then I glorify God for the teacher he was to me."

There are occasional great moments that fleetingly capture the essence of something felt, but which words fail to adequately express. For myself, a serendipitous moment took place at the Thanksgiving Service for Canon Jim Glennon. Following eulogies, readings and sermons, we stood to sing the final hymn. At the first lines of the chorus, a brave soul at the front lifted hands in praise to God—one has to remember that this was in the Cathedral! All nearby followed suit.

Then sings my soul, my Saviour God to thee
How great thou art, how great thou art!
Then sings my soul, my Saviour God to thee,
How great thou art, how great thou art!

I, too, joined the paean, and lifting my hands there was a feeling of heartfelt gratitude for the bold faith, spiritual insight, prayerfulness and loving-kindness that Canon Jim Glennon demonstrated throughout his life. Lifting hands in praise outwardly expresses an inward heart attitude. It's a bold action, one that causes eyebrows to be raised, and which, in any Cathedral, seems out of place.

It seemed to me, the lifting of our hands was a metaphor for Jim Glennon's life. His was an inner posture, a stance whereupon he fixed his eyes on the risen, living Lord, to whom all things were possible. To all who came within the sphere of his influence and teaching he directed their gaze upward to the King. Equally, he encouraged the wounded in body, mind and spirit to lift hands in thanksgiving for the great work of the Cross, and for the words of Christ they could rely on. It was not always an understood or popular stance, but he never wavered in it.

Moses, among the greatest men of God, lifted his hands at a time of crisis. He stood in the gap interceding to God on behalf of Israel. Joshua overcame the enemy for the reason that Moses' hands remained steady until sunset. Jim Glennon's hands remained steady, not just for a day but for a lifetime. He stood in the gap for the sick, sorrowing, wounded people of the world. In old age, even though he tired, he remained vigilant, doggedly determined to intercede and win spiritual battles for the many. Genuine love is always concerned to ask what it can give, rather than what it can seek for itself. Jim Glennon's gaze was always upward and outward, always seeking for the fulfilment of love's expression. In Sydney, Melbourne, and throughout Australia, in the UK and the United States, people are the recipients of the deep love of Christ made known in Canon Jim Glennon. How can we not feel deep gratitude, and how can we not lift up hands in thanks and praise to God?

At the time when Jesus entered Jerusalem there was the short, glorious moment when humanity acknowledged Him for who He was. The Pharisees asked that it be stopped. Jesus said, "If they keep quiet, the stones will cry out". There are also moments when we, too, need to acknowledge those who, by their exemplary life, cause us to lift heart, hand and voice in praise of God. The stones may well cry out if we do not do so!

Rev Roger Rich, Rector of Southern Cross Ministries—St. Paul's Anglican Church, North Caulfield, Melbourne.

The second tribute is brief. I produce it here exactly as it was given to me in a note just after Jim had died. It was written by a lady who came to the healing service Jim held at St. Mary's. The spelling and grammar are those of a newcomer to Australia.

I come to St. Mary's Healing Service a year ago and Canon Glennon ask my name I only told him once and I was suppressed how remembered each and every one of our names And he knew who was missing the next time I come he said to me three times how much he missed me.

And ones I was very sick with chest pain I ringed him up would you please pray for me than his prayer was so powerful when I called the ambulance by the time they come there was no pain. They checked my heart and bloodpresher everything was OK. I thank God for him and I will miss him greatly. I can only say he was a man of God and I loved his teachin and tried to put into practice. We lost our father there is non like him. He is with Jesus for ever Thank you Father Thank you Jesus, Thank you Holy Spirit.

Rosa Szittner.

What a beautiful letter!

Obituary

Feared by some, misunderstood by many, loved by thousands, but mightily used by God, was the epitaph stated at his funeral to describe Canon Jim Glennon, founder of the famed healing services in St. Andrew's Cathedral. Glennon, known in some circles as "the man who made religious healing respectable" was a larger-than-life, sometimes controversial figure who shunned personal publicity yet gained national and international attention because of his devotion to a topic once considered the domain of fringe bodies and quackery. Some called him "the healer" a term he thought should be reserved for God. When questioned by the curious he would say "He did it, not me" and point to the sky. He considered himself the "instrument" once comparing himself to a surgeon's scalpel.

Over 28 years and a further 16 years after formal retirement, it is estimated some 500,000 people participated at one time or another in Glennon's healing ministry at home and abroad. He (or to be precise, the Holy Spirit through him) is credited with several hundred "cures" though as with others of his calling the degree of evidence is contested.

Perhaps with this in mind those present at his funeral were offered data on two widely quoted cases in which Glennon was involved. Both occurred during overseas trips shortly after his formal retirement from the Cathedral staff.

The first in London in 1989 involved Julie Sheldon, a dancer with the Royal Ballet who was a victim of dystonia, a neuro-muscular disease that left her curled up in a foetal position and close to death. Her apparent total cure was described by doctors as inexplicable!

The second in Florida in 1992 involved Don Jaeger who was suffering amyotrophic lateral sclerosis, also known as Lou Gehrig's disease after a star baseballer of that name. After being prayed over by Glennon, combined with physical therapy, the once totally crippled man went snow skiing. A doctor at the Cleveland Clinic, which specialises in the condition, says of the former patient "It's as if he never had it."

Ordinary visitors to St. Andrew's Cathedral saw in Glennon a welcoming figure with a fatherly stoop. He exuded warmth but preferred to remain slightly aloof from those he counselled or over whom he prayed. Possibly, like hospital nurses he could not afford to be too close to patients. He was invariably polite, although when occasion demanded, he could be surprisingly blunt. Telephone discussions always ended with the words 'God bless you and goodbye.'

He suffered for much of his life with an eye condition, which caused mild facial disfigurement. Many found this evidence of his own physical weakness comforting. Critics used it as a barb. 'Physician heal thyself' was a comment sometimes heard.

Being a single man without family responsibilities the Cathedral became his life. He would joke about this and that his brothers and other male relatives were mostly single or without children. A cousin in Melbourne who had a son was the exception. In later years worried about family lineage Jim would ring his cousin enquire about the young man's health then follow up with "Ah, but has he got a girl friend yet?"

Alan Gill, *Sydney Morning Herald*, July 13, 2005.

Jim Glennon had friends in North America who not only have warm and bright memories of him but who have taken his ideas "on board" as he used to put it. Canon Jim took the great truths of the here-and-now Kingdom of God and showed us how to pray so that these truths could dominate our innermost being to the glory of God. For him the orthodox doctrine of the Atonement was a barrier-breaking reality for dealing with every kind of problem addressed by the broad themes of scriptural promise.

> The influence of this great man of God, and great Australian, will be felt for generations, and we are deeply thankful for his life. It would be fitting for all of us now to go forward with the determination expressed in one of Canon's own prayers which reads, in part, as follows: "By your grace I will now walk in your way all my life until it comes my turn to stand before you and receive the crown of everlasting life. In the name of the Father and of the Son and of the Holy Spirit, Amen."

The Committee of North American Friends of
Canon Jim Glennon, the Rev Robert Godley,
the Rev Paul Zahl, Richard Scott-Ram and John B Donovan.

Jim's resting place is two-fold; half of his ashes are interred in the chancel at St. Mary's Anglican Church Waverley. The following words are inscribed on the plaque:-

Interred here are the ashes of
Canon Alfred James (Jim) Glennon AM *1920–2005*
Honorary Priest in this Place
who brought enlightenment of the Bible to this Parish
through God's Ministry of Healing.
Forever rest in peace good and faithful servant.

The other half of his ashes are interred at St. Andrew's Cathedral in Sydney. His final resting place here is alongside the choir pews since he was the Precentor from 1957 to 1962. The following words are inscribed on this plaque:-

In loving memory of Canon Alfred James Glennon AM
1920–2005
who served on the Cathedral staff for 33 years
and who founded the Healing Ministry in the Cathedral
in 1960—Jesus the same yesterday and today …

Part Two

The Charismatic in the non-Charismatic Church

⟹◈⟸

J im had some very sound and balanced views about denominations within the Christian Church. He would often express the view that the worst thing the Christian Church ever did was to divide into Catholic and Protestant since the Reformation did nothing to reform the Church or unite Christians. As Jim put it "the last was worse than the first" since it has done nothing through the ages to unite Christendom but to divide it even further. His description of himself as an Anglican was that he was a Charismatic, Evangelical Sacramentalist. He tried to maintain a "balance" in his understanding of these things, and was very supportive of all denominations, even though some had again divided in more recent times.

Jim's attitude towards the different churches was that all churches (by which he meant local churches as well as denominations) have their weaknesses as well as their strengths. The point he made was that, if a person leaves a church after some years because of a weakness, and then relocates to another, initially because of its perceived strength, then often the last stage is again worse than the first. Ultimately, weaknesses will surface because they all have weaknesses as they all have strengths.

In 1982 Jim gave a talk on this subject. He called it "The Charismatic in the non-Charismatic Church." His papers give no indication as to the exact date or the occasion on which it was presented. It speaks volumes about his loyalty to, and respect for, the Sydney Diocese of the Anglican Church from which he could so easily have split. It is reprinted here as it was originally transcribed from his spoken address, with little or no editing.

I came into the Renewal Movement, or the Charismatic Movement as it was then more commonly called, in Easter 1961 through the ministry of Agnes Sanford, and so I have been charismatic since that time, which is twenty-one years and have all that time been at St. Andrew's Cathedral which, for the purposes of what I am talking about, could be described as a non-charismatic church. And so I know something from the personal point of view of what I am speaking about.

What I will say cannot help but be somewhat subjective and autobiographical; at the same time I hope that what I have to say will have a general application and I will try and make it like that as well as talking about my own personal situation.

It is a subject that affects many people because we do not choose the parish where we belong. So, frequently we come into Renewal and find we are in a parish where these things are not only not emphasised but could be actively opposed. And so I would think the interest in this subject is widespread both for us and for others.

I realise that there may be more things to say than I am going to say. It may well be that you would have a contribution, certainly an experience in this area, that will be valid and important to share and I hope that there will be time for us to have some discussion at the end where your own insights and experiences might come into focus.

The first thing I want to say, and again it is really before I begin to talk about the charismatic and the non-charismatic church, is that when we come to Renewal I believe it is absolutely vital that you stay in your own church. So often, that has not been the case, and if you leave your mainline church (and I am not just talking about the Anglican Church), if you leave whatever is your mainline denominational church and join a Charismatic/Pentecostal group that may well be set up for that kind of purpose, I think you will find that the last stage is worse than the first. Because, apart from anything else, you will tend to find both in yourself and in the group you join—I am talking about leaving the church and joining a Charismatic body—you will tend to find that both you and they over-emphasise certain things to justify what you have done, and what they have done, and you will immediately have a lack of balance that will ultimately be self-defeating. You will tend to find, and I am sorry to say this, and I am not intending to be at all hurtful or insulting to the Pentecostal churches, far be it, but you will tend to find that those kind of church bodies are here today and gone tomorrow. You will also find they have a reputation and a reality of splitting themselves because, once people leave a church body because there is something about it that they do not like, it will not be long before they find there is something else they do not like, and that principle permeates the body.

I remember meeting the Pentecostal minister of a church in a country town—a large country town—and I said to him (we were going flying together) "How are things in your church?" "Oh," he said, "We have just had a split." But he said that in much the same kind of way as we might say, "It's a fine day today." It did not seem to worry him in the least—it was taken for granted, and I think the Pentecostal church would be known more for its splits and divisions than perhaps any other Christian body in Christendom, and I am sorry to say that (and if I'm wrong I will more than withdraw and apologise) but I think that would be a point of view commonly held by at least some people.

I will be a little more personal still and say you take the Christian Faith Centre that was at Crows Nest Sydney for a number of years after Renewal came to Sydney, largely made up of ex-Anglicans and ex-denominational people from other church bodies, and I say again they are here today and gone tomorrow. The last stage is worse than the first.

The other reason why you should not leave your mainline church is a more positive reason and that is—you will leave your parent body un-reformed. You will leave your parent body un-renewed.

They will adopt a negative attitude towards you personally, and what you stand for, because you have left. It will harden their heart against what you stand for. I repeat—you leave the parent body un-reformed and un-renewed. I think this is a totally untenable position for more reasons than one—not the least of which is your own personal welfare—that you should leave your own church and belong to some other body where your new conviction and experience will have comparatively free rein. And so I want to talk in a positive way about a person who has come into Renewal and who has chosen to remain within his or her mainline church.

The first thing I believe you should do is to go to your own minister and tell him/her what has happened. Tell your minister you have come into Renewal. Make an appointment to see him/her. Do not try and speak to them as the congregation is filing out after the service. It is amazing the things people think they can talk to you about there. I was trained by Bryan Green for the Pastoral side of ministry and that is one thing he would never allow—someone to monopolise him as the congregation was going out. If someone wanted to talk, which is quite right and good, he would say, "Do you mind waiting?" and, when he had said goodbye to everybody, then he would give time to this person who had a question to ask. But, even so, I want to say that if you want to share this with your minister—and I advise you to do that—make an appointment. Go to the Rectory and spend time with him/her quietly and meaningfully and share with them what has happened. I think, if you will do that, you will first of all find that they will be positive about your experience and will be willing to listen to you. I remember when I came into Renewal, at some time after that and not straightaway, I went to Archbishop Loane, who is my Rector you might say, as I am at the Cathedral, and told him about my experience.

I will always remember what he said—it came to me as a surprise because I did not have this in mind when I went to see him. He said, "I am so glad you told me. I do not want to hear that from someone else." If he had heard that Jim Glennon had come into something or other from someone else, he would have felt negative about this. He would have thought, why doesn't he come to me himself?

And so I got off to a good positive start with the Archbishop and he listened to my experience and was warm and approving up to a certain point and prayed with me at the end of our conversation. Now, he said to me something which I have followed carefully as people have come to the Cathedral and the Healing Service. He said, "I must ask that you do not make a charismatic emphasis in the Cathedral." Now this was very disappointing to me. I had come into this marvellous experience. I wanted to share it with others, and here is my minister, if I might so describe the Archbishop (he is in charge of the Cathedral over the Dean), telling me I am not to make a charismatic emphasis in the Cathedral and, indeed, when I invited the Archbishop to come to the Healing Service some time later (he will not mind me saying this, I trust) he sent a message saying, "I hope no-one will speak in tongues." And so he was still wanting to be assured that this would not be part of what went on in the Healing Service. I have been loyal to the Archbishop in that respect, and will remain loyal to those instructions until they are altered.

This introduces the first main point that I want to make—that we are to be subject to the headship of our church, and that means being willing to accept something that is different to what you yourself would like to do. That is what being subject to the head means.

A woman came to see me not so very long ago and said, "Oh Canon Glennon, I want to submit to your headship". And I said, "Well, that's very nice." I had not asked her to come. I had not given her the impression that I wanted her to submit to my headship, and so I said to her, "Well, that's very nice but what if I say something different to what is your idea about things?" "Oh," she said, "I will have to think about that", and she got out of my office as quickly as she could without falling down, and I have never seen her since.

And so you see, being subject to someone's headship means that you are willing to accept their admonition, their advice, their instruction, even if it is different to what you want it to be. I have heard people say, and I have heard people say this in the Renewal Movement, "Oh, I will be subject to so and so provided they have the same experience as I have or they have the same principles as I have". That is fine, but life is not like that and it means we must be subject to the headship where God has put us, and it might be a different headship to what we ourselves would like, in the sense that this person has a different experience, or lacks the experience, that we ourselves have.

Now, over the years I have often chafed at the bit because of the restriction that His Grace put upon me and more than once I have yearned to get away and be in a place where I could have a release of the Spirit, as far as I am concerned personally, and in the expression of my ministry. But, as time has gone by, I have become increasingly comfortable with my position—I never saw that this would be an advantage—but have realised as time has gone by that what maturity I may have, what maturity and balance the Healing Ministry in the Cathedral may have, comes directly from having restraints put upon me by the headship. True it is that we do not speak in tongues, and we do not have interpretation, and we do not have other manifestations of the Spirit which are glorious and necessary, valid, and play a vital part, but [in] everything that I do and say, and [in] everything that is done and said in the Healing Ministry, I have got something in my mind which says, "I wonder what the Archbishop would say; I wonder what the Dean would say; I wonder what the Chapter would say", and they have on one or two occasions expressed their disagreement with what I have done or said.

In the long run, that is a very healthy situation to be in, because you are subject to other people who may not have the same point of view as you have, and while you may chafe at the bit, in the long run, what maturity and balance you have, will come from that situation.

One of the very worst things that can happen to a Spirit-filled person is that they are subject, or they subject themselves, to the manifestations of the Spirit. So, because they affirm that the Spirit says this or that, they do this or that, and individualism runs riot. This especially happens in the honeymoon time of being filled with the Spirit, and they will say, "I would not do this in the natural, therefore it is right that I should do it". I remember once, a clergyman (and I will say no more than that), a mature clergyman was filled with the Spirit and he was saying the Spirit has told me to do this, and the Spirit has told me to do that, and he was creating a

164

lot of problems. I was coming back from having conducted a mission in another State and I made a special detour to go and see him because I thought, well, he might not listen to others but he might listen to me. I am filled with the Spirit. But I found he would not listen to me either and that is so often the case. The person who is filled with the Spirit and has a marvellous experience of the reality of God, and says he is going to do what he believes God has told him to do—I tell you, if a person does that, he will find that the last stage is always worse than the first because the Bible says, let the prophet speak but let the others judge. No-one can get up and say, "Thus says the Lord. Brothers, you do it," because the Bible says—let the others judge. It is not a word from the Lord unless it is corporately approved. Even then the Body can be wrong in their judgment but obviously there is much less likelihood of the Body being wrong than the individual being wrong. And so there is every good reason why we need to subject ourselves to a headship, or if you like a corporate judgment, that will assess what we are doing, or saying, and that it is scriptural.

This brother would not listen to me or anyone else—suffice it to say his last stage was worse than the first. The one thing that I am more convinced about than perhaps any other, is the need for us to be corporate, is the need for us to be subject to others, is the need for us to listen to others who may not even have the same point of view as we have. Stay in your church, be subject to the headship, be concerned to do things in a corporate way and then you are in a position where God can use you, given time.

Now, assuming we have subjected ourselves in a meaningful way to the headship of our church and all that that means, then let us go on and demonstrate by our life what it means to be filled with the Spirit so that we are people whom others may well copy. Once at the Cathedral we had a Catechist and he was a typical Moore College product as far as these things are concerned (and I am not saying that disagreeably) he just didn't go along with Renewal and he was at the Cathedral. I did not have a great deal of contact with him at all, but I knew what his position was and I respected it, and he knew what my position was and never the twain shall meet, but when he left to go to Western Australia he sought me out and he said, "There is just one thing I would like to say to you Canon

Glennon. I have been at the Cathedral twelve months and I have been able to see people and observe people and see what goes on, and I would just like to say that it is my considered opinion that the people at the Cathedral who are most active in worship, who are most meaningful in their Christian service, who are most acceptable in their personal behavior, are the people involved in the Charismatic Movement." In other words, they were people who were demonstrating quietly, indirectly if you like, something that made them admired by someone who was not involved and, if you like, was even opposed to what Renewal meant. To use a vulgar expression, it was important for us to keep our nose clean.

People are observing us all the time and they need to be able to say of us, as they reflect on us in depth, that the experience he or she has drawn on is meaningful to them — I see a change in their life. They are demonstrating this in the face of the congregation, in their devotion to our Lord, their regularity at worship, and their sacrificial service, and in all things about them and about their ministry. If you are filled with the Spirit, let your minister realise that, as time goes by, you are the most loyal parishioner, you are the most active worker and that you are behind him in every good way, and let your fellow church members feel from their contact with you that you are someone who they can love and respect and look up to and want to emulate. What a marvellous opportunity we have of demonstrating, not just by trying to win people to being filled with the Spirit, but demonstrating the results of being filled with the Spirit in our worship and in our church life.

To begin with — it is not so apparent now, thank goodness — but people involved in Renewal were something of a divisive influence. They were all the time trying to dragoon someone else into this experience, and induce them to speak in tongues, and again so often the last stage was worse than the first. If you are persecuted for your Christian position, make sure that you are being persecuted because you are witnessing to the Lord Jesus. There can be an over-emphasis about things of the Spirit. There cannot be an over-emphasis about things of the Lord Jesus Christ. There can be an equal fault if there is an under-emphasis about things of the Spirit. That is another story, but I am only wanting to say let those who are filled with the Spirit glorify Jesus, that they may be examples for everyone else to follow, and that people look upon you with respect and with acceptance and love.

I now come to the bottom line. We stay in our church for a positive reason—that we may enable the church to be renewed. That will not be done by running around this person or that, and laying hands on them that they be filled with the Spirit, or be healed. Now, your church will be renewed because of prayer, but more than that, the Spirit will be poured out when, because you are in the situation when no one will listen to you, nothing can be done humanly speaking, yet you have a conviction born of God as far as these things of the Spirit are concerned—you are in the position where you can do nothing else except depend on God more. The Bible says, "When we are weak we are strong". When you are holed up with God, and only God can provide this blessing, and you in the natural are brought to the end of your tether, then there is a release of the Spirit, and that is the blessing of God that does work. That is the Holy Spirit reality that renews the Church.

Ultimately, as far as I am concerned personally, I have come to the conclusion that the other hill somewhere else only looks greener. If I cannot make a go of the Christian position where I am, if I cannot lead my present church to Renewal I am not going to do any better some place else. I am only having myself on. You know, although I sometimes want to be some place else where there is liberty and so on, I have come to the conclusion that no-one is going to get me out of St. Andrew's Cathedral unless I am put out, because to be in the position where you have only got God to depend on, is always the best position to be in for your own personal sanctification, and to have the blessing of God, and for others to have the blessing of God. Do you follow me?

It isn't easy; it can be heartbreaking. It is not easy to die to your own self-consciousness. I tell you it's hurtful and it's painful. St. Paul says "I die daily", and that was the secret of his ministry. That is why the Holy Spirit was poured out upon St. Paul and through Paul, throughout his life. He said he had so much in permitted difficulties he had got nothing else to do but to depend on God, and God only does the work.

Now there is no virtue on my own part. It is just that God uses the permitted difficulties so that we are not trusting in ourselves but in God, as it says in 2 Corinthians 1:9; and when we are brought by the circumstances so we are trusting not in ourselves but in God, then, and only then, is the Holy Spirit truly poured out. That is the suffering church, but that is the powerful church. I could develop this subject—I would like to spend the whole evening talking on that line. And, when you get that right, then something is going to happen from God to renew your church.

I want to give an illustration of this before I further develop my address. Twelve years ago, following the first National Evangelical Anglican Congress in Monash University in Melbourne, a committee was formed by the Synod of the Diocese of Sydney to enquire into the Healing Ministry and the Renewal Movement and I, with others, was a member of that committee. We met for two years, and, as far as I was concerned, it was the most distressing time of my whole life. There was an argument from beginning to end. The committee was heavily weighted in favour of those who were non-charismatic, and I am not an argumentative person, and I found it distressing in the extreme. Bishop Reid was taking doctors around the Diocese and holding meetings and debunking the Healing Ministry, and the report that came out on both sides of the question just polarised the whole Diocese on these matters. In the Cathedral School, which is cheek by jowl with the Cathedral itself, there was a public meeting where the boys were paraded and got medical people in to debunk the Healing Ministry, etc etc etc.

That was twelve years ago, and I know something of the distress and the heartache and the division that can happen over these things, and I felt very much an outsider to what was going on—and clergy of course, they get the Diocesan message and they are fearful of doing anything else anyway, and it put many men in that position and has lasted until this day. But, when you are in a position where the permitted circumstances give you no alternative but to depend on God more, there is a constant outflow of the Holy Spirit. As the Bible says, if it is of men it will come to nothing. If it is of God no one can stand against it.

Last year they planned on having another National Evangelical Anglican Congress in the Monash University. In case you do not know, it is the "true blue" Evangelical Anglicanism and to my astonishment I was officially approached and was asked would I

168

be on the Executive Committee. I did not know why and so I made some enquiries and I was told plainly, "We know what your position is — you are involved in Renewal and you are involved in the Healing Ministry and we do not want any more division on these matters. We want you to be on the Executive Committee which will plan the whole conference". So I was.

As a result, one of the four themes was Renewal in the Spirit. Every day at the Conference there was a theme. One of those days and one of those themes was Renewal in the Spirit. We, the Executive Committee of which I was a member, imported Michael Cassidy from South Africa who gave the paper, and I am not exaggerating when I say it was the celebration day of the Conference and Bishop Witt, an Anglo-Catholic Bishop from the Diocese of Brisbane gave his testimony about being filled with the Spirit and when he, in the Anglo-Catholic Diocese said that, it had meant as a result he had to walk a Calvary road, because those men who had walked with him so far, walked with him no longer. When he concluded his testimony and sat down the whole Congress rose to its feet and applauded him to the echo. It was the celebration day of the National Evangelical Congress.

There were also papers given on the Healing Ministry and those I heard were very good indeed. I was asked to conduct workshops on the Healing Ministry, and more people wanted to come than they could accommodate, and they were very good workshops indeed. On the last night of the Congress, after Bishop John Reid, who was the Chairman, had spoken, we happened to meet outside the lecture theatre, and his words to me were, "You must be very happy with what has happened." I said, "Yes, John, I am." Wisdom is justified of her children. If it is of God, in the long run, if we are faithful, it will be justified by God.

And so you see, I believe that if we will stay within our church we will submit ourselves to the headship — we will be people who are a reasonable expression of what we profess and the permitted circumstances give us no alternative but that we are depending on God more. The Holy Spirit will do His own work.

Now, in the Diocese of Sydney which has not been renowned for its acceptance of these things — rather the contrary — David Watson, who is perhaps the leader of the Renewal Movement in

England these days, has not only been here and preached in the Cathedral with great acceptance, warmly supported by Archbishop Loane, but Bishop Reid has been wanting to get him back and take missions in various parts of the Diocese, and it is only financial things that is preventing it, because David Watson wants to bring his big team of twelve people and it is a very expensive thing—we just cannot pay the bill. Terry Fullam has been here three times at least, and he spoke in the Cathedral Healing Service on his last visit, and I made it an opportunity to invite our new Archbishop [Robinson] to come and hear him and afterwards I had arranged a supper party in the vestry for Terry Fullam to meet Archbishop and Mrs Robinson and different members of our own committee; and I was in the Chapter House with the other folk and we had a supplementary address there and when I came back to the vestry thinking they would have had a lovely time in the supper party meeting Terry Fullam, I said "Where's Terry Fullam, where's the Archbishop?" "Oh" they said, "they are closeted in the Dean's vestry. They have been talking together for an hour. We haven't seen them.".

I went to Bishopscourt two nights later to one of the dinner parties for the clergy, and His Grace greeted me with the words, "I am so glad I met Terry Fullam and talked with him". And Terry Fullam will be the great leader in America as far as the Renewal Movement is concerned in the Episcopal Church. Things are changing, and I have said to brother Allen that if Terry Fullam comes back again let us go to the Archbishop and say, "Your Grace, the Reverend Terry Fullam is willing to come. Would you like to sponsor his ministry? Would you like to make the arrangements?"

Before, this would have been impossible, but now we are at the point where these things are being understood, accepted and used. What changes can happen over ten years! And that is the point I am wanting to make; that one has to take a long-range approach as far as these things are concerned. You take the Healing Ministry. At the last Lambeth Conference in 1978 all the Archbishops and Bishops of the Anglican Communion worldwide issued an Encyclical Letter and this is what all the Bishops of the Anglican Church said about the Healing Ministry.

*"We affirm that healing the sick in Christ's name is as much a part
of the Good News of the Gospel as the forgiveness of sins. To neglect
this aspect of ministry is to diminish our part in Christ's redemptive
activity. It must be an essential part of liturgical reform."*

So in our new Anglican Prayer Book there are marvellous prayers
which we use every week in the Healing Service in praying for
the sick, that they be raised up and in a Supplementary Order of
Service which is a little bit different because (I will not trouble you
with the explanation) they could only revise the Book of Common
Prayer in terms of those references, and other things like the Anointing of the Sick had to be done in a supplementary way. Plans are
already afoot and have been accepted by a committee appointed
by the Standing Committee of this Diocese to accept the Order of
Service that will ultimately have official sanction in the Anglican
Church in Australia to making specific reference and approval for
the Laying on of Hands, Anointing with Oil and the Healing of
the Sick in exactly the same way as we have been doing at St. Andrew's Cathedral for twenty-two years.

So, if you stay in your church, be subject to the headship, be the
kind of people that God will use despite our faults, let the circumstances enable you to depend on God more, and, given time, the
Holy Spirit will do the work. We are on the winning side. It is of
God. Praise the Lord!

Now, let me say just one thing more before I close. While I say,
stay in your church, and I have given some areas of reference that
will make that meaningful, you may well need to belong to a supplementary group where the things of the Spirit will be stirred up.
With all things in life you can have use, abuse, non-use. You can
have a most meaningful experience of being filled with the Spirit,
but if you do not do the things that will enable you to progress in
these things, it will die through disuse. While you will not get that
help in a non-charismatic church you need to belong to a supplementary group where you will grow in these things.

Now, I follow the guidance of the Archbishop about not making
a charismatic emphasis in the Cathedral but I feel completely free
to go to, and be a part of, and indeed take a lead in a supplementary group where these things have a meaningful and free expres-

sion. There has got to be a balance in these things and as far as I can imagine (it has never happened) but as far as I can imagine, if I was told you cannot do that, I would say, "Oh yes I can."

Within my church I am subject to the headship, but there is a limit. We also have to obey God rather than men and it is very interesting that although I am very loyal to the Cathedral position, I feel free to have a wider ministry in these areas and the Cathedral authorities have never said "No" to me in any shape or form. Provided you are loyal to your church setting, I believe you will be given liberty in other respects, do you see? That is most important. Provided they know you are loyal, then in the Anglican Church you will find there is liberty for you to develop these things in ways that are right and needful because you very much need instruction. You very much need experience and you very much need growth in these things.

I remember a lady who I know. She and her husband were helpful to me when I was writing my book. She was filled with the Spirit and she had a marvellous gift of prophecy. I have never heard anybody (and I do not care who it is) who had such a marvellous gift of prophecy. I said to her, "Joyce, have you always had this gift of prophecy? Is it something the Lord endowed you with?" "Oh, no," she said, "when I first began, I felt God calling me to that ministry. When I first began to open my mouth and give a word of prophecy, quite frankly as I look back on it, it was just my own good ideas with Amen on the end, but because I had faith to open my mouth, God used my faith so that more and more it wasn't my own good ideas with Amen on the end; it was God's good ideas that I was speaking out."

You increase in these things—you learn how to pray. Agnes Sanford said nothing ever came out of the blue as far as her understanding of the Healing Ministry is concerned, although she ultimately became the world authority on it, and I would say the same thing about myself, for what it is worth. Nothing ever comes out of the blue. I have just worked at it. We learn how to pray in the same way as we learn how to do anything and everything. And so I share this with you. Be loyal to your church etc. But belong to a supplementary group where you will grow in the use of these things of the Spirit and that is very important.

Let me say one thing more by way of closing because I do not want it to really focus on me at all. I am not sure whether we have with us tonight Mrs. Florence Stuckey and her husband, Bo. Florence is filled with the Spirit and she has just a wonderful ministry of taking the tapes of the Lambeth Conference to do with Renewal around the clergy and others and she does this in a most prayerful and discerning way and she just knows how to get alongside them and commend the tapes to them and lend them and go back later and pick them up and have conversation, and you know there are dozens of clergy in the Diocese who are gradually getting to understand the Renewal Movement through listening to these tapes by Terry Fullam from the Lambeth Conference on Renewal. That is because someone who is filled with the Spirit is seeking to be an evangelist and in a beautiful way — gradually, slowly progressing, because so often we are seeking to overcome misunderstanding and give information that people might see things in a positive and creative way. We might not all do it in that way but you wait on the Lord and He will give you something to do for the Renewal Movement that will enable our Church to be renewed, for surely that is our goal. Praise God.

Sermon Notes

J im's sermons given at the Healing Ministry in St. Andrew's Cathedral on Wednesday nights often took the form of a series of three, with a common theme. The following three sermons were given on consecutive Wednesdays, the 8th, the 15th and the 22nd December, 1982. They are reproduced here as they were transcribed by Deaconess Gwyneth Hall and distributed to the Postal Congregation.

Three Main Themes in the Healing Ministry

(1) SEEK GOD FOR HIMSELF

Hymn: Tell out, my soul, the greatness of the Lord
Lesson: 2 Corinthians 12:1–10

I plan on giving three addresses which I have called "Three Main Themes in the Healing Ministry" and tonight I'm calling my address: "Seek God for himself". I introduce what I want to say by making the statement that there is more than one way to pray, and I'm going to talk tonight about a way to pray that is different from the usual way. Very different and very important. So important that I would say it is one of the three main themes of the Healing Ministry. It will take patience to understand this and to keep it in one's mind so it is effective, but you will be encouraged when I say that it is my view and experience that this is one of the most powerful and productive ways there is to pray.

To understand what is involved we need to have in mind first of all the usual way we pray. I could sum that up very easily and say that we believe God is helping us with our problems. That is perfectly valid, provided we are praying the prayer of faith as the prayer of faith is described in the Bible (see Mark 11:20–26). The difficulty with that regular way of praying is that it is focusing on the problem, and often it is difficult to get one's focus away from what one sees, and the burden of it. The principle of that kind of prayer is that God is behind us (as it were) and we are facing our problems. God is helping us to pray about our problems.

Now, I can explain what I am wanting to share with you tonight—this different way to pray—by saying that you need to turn around one hundred and eighty degrees. The problem is still there, but whereas it has been in front of you, now it is behind you. Whereas God had been behind you before, now you are facing towards God. Before, God was helping you with your problems. Now your problems are helping you with God! That is the difference! It means that we are reacting to our permitted difficulties by moving closer to God and depending on God more. Not praying about our difficulties but praying about God! Drawing closer to Him; drawing on Him; experiencing Father, Son and Holy Spirit. That is a very different way of praying. Let me say again: Before, God is helping us with our problems. Now our problems are helping us with God.

I haven't finished. If you are going to pray this way, you have to go a step further and seek to draw upon God for Himself, and not so that He will take your problems away, or give you healing. When Jesus said that we are to seek the Kingdom of God first and His righteousness (Matthew 6:33) He meant just what I am now saying. That we are to seek God first, meaning, we are to seek God for Himself, and not so that he will add unto us all things, that is, take away our problem. That is what that little word "first" means. Now I am not saying that this is easy to do. I am not saying that. I am saying that it is a valid thing to do. It is something we will have to apply ourselves to with patience and perseverance—till we come to the point of our problems helping us to pray about God and to seek God for Himself, and not so that He will ultimately take away our permitted difficulties.

I wonder how many of us have really prayed like that—even once. That is, to seek God for Himself. Not so that He will give us anything, except Himself. Yet that is the ultimate in prayer. That is what our relationship with God is all about. To seek God, and to seek God alone, and be filled with all the fullness of God (Ephesians 3:19). He promises to add unto us all things, but to really seek God for Himself is to seek Him for Himself and not so that he will add unto us all things.

When we get this right, two things happen. We will draw upon an experience of God. We have been seeking Him—we will receive Him, and we will know what it is to be filled with the Spirit. We will know what it is to be filled with all the fullness of God. We will know what it is to be full, pressed down, shaken together and running over (Luke 6:38) with the Spirit of God. If you seek God for Himself, you will receive God. And when you have come to the point where you are seeking God only, you will find that he adds unto you "all things" and you will have an experience of healing, an experience of your mountain being cast into the sea (Mark 11:23), an experience of answered prayer that far exceeds any other way of praying.

At an earlier time in the Healing Ministry, that is the way the ministry was exercised here, and I can still remember that the answers to prayer were perhaps greater than at any other time, or as a result of any other way of praying. I also speak with personal conviction on this matter because at an earlier time in my own life, before there was a Healing Ministry, and when I had broken down in health emotionally, I learned to pray this way. I know what it is like to get it right not once, but day by day and time by time, and well do I remember that this was the time in my life when I had, in my own small way, small way, the abundance of revelation. God revealed Himself to me time by time, and more and more and in a progressive way. And my problems which had reached paralytic proportions, were, not all at once, but spadeful by spadeful, cast into the sea. Those difficulties which had brought me to the end of my tether, I now not only do not have, but I cannot recall ever having had, because when God heals it is as though you had never had the problem at all.

Let us pray: Our loving Father, we would depend on you more. We would react to our difficulties so we seek you, and you only for yourself, and we do that now, more and more, through Christ our Lord, Amen.

(2) WHAT YOU CONFESS, YOU POSSESS

Hymn: Standing on the promises of God
Lesson: Matthew 12:33–37

As we come to the end of a year of activity and ministry I thought it would be valuable to try and sum up some of the main things that we emphasise in the Healing Service. This is why I have called these addresses: "Three Main Themes in the Healing Ministry". Tonight my address is: "What you confess, you possess".

One of the things that is fundamental to Christian experience is that we know what God has promised to provide, and that we exercise repentance and faith and obedience that we might have these provisions in point of fact. This means that we accept the promised blessings of God so we believe we receive them, both for ourselves and for others. This means that we are accepting the answers that God provides. We are confessing the answer that God provides with our words and from our hearts. Because we confess it, we possess it.

It will add point to what I am saying and sharing with you, for me to also say—and this again is a continuing theme in Healing Ministry teaching—that so often what we confess (and what we possess) is not the answer that God provides, but the problem that has come from the sin of the world. Of course the difficulty is that the problem is what we see. The problem is what we have. The problem is what gives rise to the anxiety and the apprehension and the fear. But a fundamental tenet of the Christian position is that we are to walk not by sight but by faith. Faith is not what you see; it is what you hope for and what you believe you receive so that you do not doubt in your heart. The point I am making is that we are all confessing something and we are all possessing something, whether we know it or not, whether we like it or not. And so often we are confessing and possessing the difficulties. What we are to confess and possess are the answers and the provisions that God makes.

More than that, Jesus said that we are to believe we have received these things, so we do not doubt in our hearts (Mark 11:23). It is not enough to confess the answer that God provides in a fifty-fifty way. So often we have a foot in both camps, and this is why it doesn't work in the way that it needs to work. It will help us to be wholehearted in what we do if we accept the provision of God like we accept Christ. At least, if you have that in your mind, you will have an understanding and a prayer activity that will be something you are used to and can put into practice. Accept all the promises of God like you accept Christ so they are what you affirm by faith and therefore in praise. As you affirm the promises of God by faith you will increasingly experience them by sight.

I can only say that in my prayer activity I am constantly seeking to switch over from confessing the problem to confessing the answer, for myself and for others. I am constantly seeking to perfect my confession of God's answer, so that I possess it—for myself and for others.

Apply this to yourselves and in different areas. I was at an evening last night, and they talked about confessing the miracles of God in our congregational life. It should be like this in every congregational life, of course. Let us confess, and possess, the miracles of God—not just during the Healing Service—it includes that, of course—but day by day, and time by time, and person by person. Let us confess the conversion of other people, so they possess it. Our faith will enable them to have faith. Let us confess the fullness of the Holy Spirit for others, individually and collectively, so that because of our faith, they will have faith. What you confess, you possess. It applies where you apply it! But I come back to my earlier point—you are going to confess something—and so often what we are confessing is the problem. That is why we have got the problem, and that is why others have got their problems. Let us confess the answer and we will possess that. Praise God!

I would like to give an illustration. We have been praying for rain. I commend the Premier of Queensland for giving a lead in his office as Premier, by calling upon the people of Queensland to pray for rain. We praise God that, as a result of that, there has been rain in Queensland. I want to give an illustration from my own experience to encourage everybody to confess and possess rain for our country. Nothing could be more needful. In one part we have been told about, they have had a drought for four years—until they prayed for rain!

I was once in Gilgandra, in the western part of NSW, taking a mission and they were in drought. The country was brown and dry and cracked, and they asked me would we pray for rain in the mission. I didn't pray straight away. I have learned that it is good to let the Spirit be stirred up before you commit yourself to prayer. The mission began on a Sunday and I didn't pray for rain until the following Thursday, as far as the mission meetings were concerned. When I felt we had reached this point, I asked everyone to stand, and I prayed something like this: "Lord, Jesus said whatsoever things you desire, when you pray, believe that you have received them, so that you do not doubt and they will be yours. We now accept rain for this locality. We confess it, and by faith we possess it, in Jesus' Name."

We all prayed, we all believed, we all confessed it. We accepted it like we accepted Christ. That was the Thursday. Friday the skies were like brass. Saturday, again the skies were like brass. Sunday morning, I was speaking in one of the churches, and I said to the organist: "Oh, we're believing for rain," and she said: "It won't rain. It hasn't rained for eighteen months!" Well, I didn't get much help there! I assumed she hadn't been to the mission. I disciplined myself not to say: "Oh dear me" but "Praise the Lord!"

We came out from the Church and I saw a small cloud in the sky, no bigger than a man's hand, and I praised God for that small cloud. We came to the mission service that night in the Town Hall. Still no rain, but we were confessing rain by faith. After the mission service we locked up, were about to move away, and down came the rain. And it rained, and it rained. We left the next day. We just got out before the roads were closed. I shall never forget it! You see, the whole mission congregation was believing. They confessed it, and they possessed it. Faith gave way to sight.

I say again: what you confess, you possess.

Let us pray: Our loving Father, we would accept your blessings promised in your Word, for ourselves and for others, and we would so confess them that we possess them, in Jesus' Name, Amen.

(3) MOMENT BY MOMENT FAITH

<hr/>

Hymn: Angels from the realms of glory
Lesson: Luke 18:1–8

It is lovely to see the Cathedral filled with people for I cannot see a vacant seat. I thank God for the congregation we have, not only tonight, but week by week.

Coming to the end of this year of ministry, I have given three addresses, of which this is the third, called "Three Main Themes in the Healing Ministry". The first night I said that we are to seek God for Himself, and last week I said that what you confess, you possess. Tonight I have called my address "Moment by moment faith".

So that I may come to what I have to share with you tonight, let me begin by saying that the principle of prayer, as I believe it to be, is that we are first to know the promises of God. That is what the New Testament is all about. It is about the great and precious promises that God has made. The promises of God reveal the will of God. The Bible says we are to be partakers of the promise of Christ in the Gospel (Ephesians 3:6). The first thing to know is what God wants us to have. The second thing is that we are to believe we have received the promises of God so that we do not doubt, Jesus said (Mark 11:23). Now I am assuming this. I refer to it because of what I want to go on and say. It is a theme that is developed regularly at this Service.

Once you know the promises of God as revealed in the broad themes of the New Testament, and once you are believing that you have received these things so that you do not doubt in your heart—there is the need for ongoing, moment by moment faith. I don't tire of saying that when I accepted the promise of Salvation and by faith believed on Christ, nothing happened. So I went back to the Rector and said: "Rector, but it's not working." And he said to me: "You have to have moment by moment faith." And I remember how I went away and disciplined my mind by affirming God's blessing in my life in a moment by moment way.

The Bible says faith is what you hope for; it is not what you have (Hebrews 11:1). And "without faith it is impossible to please God."[16] That means there has to be a time when we are thanking God for His blessing before we have it in reality. But if you get it right, so that you are affirming the promise of God by faith in a moment by moment way, you will find increasingly that faith gives way to sight—like my conversion experience—"first the blade, then the ear..."[17] That means you are more and more experiencing it in blessed reality as far as your life is concerned.

That is how you exercise faith for all the promises of God. You believe you have received them. Almost always this has to be followed by a moment by moment faith affirmation until faith gives way to sight. That is what I am talking about tonight.

Part of what I want to say now is that this is what is meant by fasting. We don't talk about fasting very much, and more's the pity. By fasting we mean the person chooses to do without food for a period of time. To begin with they may well be miserable because they are conscious that they have done without their meal, but if they will have patience, after a couple of days they will be quite unconscious that they are hungry. And if they react to the physical sensation that fasting gives so that as a result they are exercising moment by moment faith in the promises of God, that is what fasting is all about and is intended to do. That is the purpose it serves. It gives you a moment by moment reminder, stimulus or spur to be affirming the blessing of God by faith.

---

16 *Hebrews 11:6*

17 *Mark 4:28*

And once you really start to fast, it is not a burden at all. On the contrary, your faith life gets lifted up on to a new plane and life flows like a song. And far from wanting it to conclude, you only want it to continue. That is also what is meant by sacrificial prayer—a sacrifice is being made; you are creating circumstances that, rightly understood and rightly reacted to, will give you moment by moment faith. Would to God we all knew much more about fasting and ministering before the Lord (see Acts 13:2). We would have much more blessing from God than at present we have.

I want to talk about this now in the area of healing because this is the Church's Ministry of Healing. I am going to tell you an incident from my own life to help make the point and that will be a help, I trust.

I used to have an eye complaint called "iritis". It is a very painful condition and requires skilled and immediate medical help. The medical treatment, when drawn on, puts you out of action; you can't focus for as long as the treatment is being given. I know what it is like to be out of action for weeks at a time when I've had these attacks of iritis.

As time went by I decided that I would exercise faith for the healing of my iritis. It was just continuing on and, if anything, was getting worse. The first thing I noticed about it—and this is not without its interest and value—I noticed that I got iritis in October. I believe the reason was that I was anticipating this was going to happen in October. Because it happened in previous Octobers, I believed it would happen next October. I can only say I believe that is the case. The Bible says "The thing that I feared is come upon me" (Job 3:25). Anyway, be that as it may, I came to the point where I believed God had made a promise to raise me up as far as this was concerned (James 5:14,15), and then I believed I was receiving this healing. Nothing happened, but I began to discipline my mind with moment by moment faith.

Here I want to say something about the doctor. When I went to my ophthalmologist and told her I was exercising faith for the healing of the iritis I had at that particular time, she said something to me that I have never forgotten. "If you are exercising faith for healing I will give you a different treatment." It wasn't so severe; it didn't put me out of action. She said, "I've never given this treat-

186

ment before, but if you're exercising faith, I feel this is what I can do, and it is different from what I usually do."

I disciplined myself to react to the pain by affirming faith that God was healing me at that time. The pain is a rather alarming one, and so I had my spur, or reason, and I disciplined my mind to react to the pain by affirming the healing of God in a present tense kind of way. And because the pain continued on, I had a moment by moment reason to be believing God, and that is what I sought to do. And that is what I continued to do until the pain and the iritis went away. It came back again at a later time, and again I accepted healing and affirmed it with a moment by moment faith. This time the pain went away more quickly, and when it came back there was a much bigger gap between the attacks, and as I continued to react to the pain and the alarming symptoms by knowing the promise that God would raise me up and exercised faith in this moment by moment way, I reached the point where the iritis never came back again. It is now many years since I have had any trouble as far as that is concerned.

I can only ask that you be open-minded enough to try these things and put them into practice. If you want to read something, Francis MacNutt's book called *The Prayer That Heals* has a remarkable number of illustrations that bring out the point that I am making and sharing with you. The point he makes is, as you exercise moment by moment faith in a cumulative way, the blessing is there. I share this with you as something that I have found to be meaningful and effective as far as I am concerned. In other words, we need, as the lesson said, persevering faith. We must know the promises of God, we must exercise faith, and it will need a moment by moment affirmation in a continuing way. The more you get that right, the more you will find you have the healing of God in reality.

Let us pray: Our loving Father, we would have moment by moment faith in the promises of God. We would react to our difficulties so they provide that moment by moment reminder to be believing God. Thank you, Father, we do that now, in Jesus' Name, and for Jesus' sake. Amen.

Resource material

Canon Jim was responsible for a collection of resource material during his tenure at St. Andrew's Cathedral Sydney, The Healing Ministry Centre Golden Grove Ltd, and St. Mary's Church Waverley.

The material, available in printed form, DVD, CD or on cassette tape, can be used by leaders of study groups, or by those wanting to start and operate a healing ministry.

A catalogue of resource material is available from:

The Healing Ministry Centre Golden Grove Ltd
5 Forbes Street,
Newtown, NSW 2042
Australia

Phone: (02) 9557 1642
Fax: (02) 9557 1412
Email: centre@healingministrysydney.org

The catalogue can also be accessed online on The Healing Ministry Centre's website:– www.users.bigpond.com/hmcgg/centre.htm or on www.canonjimglennon.com

The Canon Jim Glennon Healing Ministry Trust

APPLYING FOR FUNDING FROM THE TRUST

The Trustees distribute earnings and interest only (not capital) from the Trust annually. Any person, church, ministry or group, may apply for funds for any new initiative which satisfies the Trust's requirement that it would extend the Kingdom of God through the ministry of healing.

The Trustees would, typically, appoint a "Relations Manager" to engage with the recipient of the Trust money in order to encourage and support the project and to ensure that it is conducted in accordance with the Deed of Trust.

Any person, church, ministry or group seeking financial support for a project meeting the guidelines should apply in writing to:

The Board of Trustees,
The Canon Jim Glennon Healing Ministry Trust
C/- The Healing Ministry Centre Golden Grove Ltd,
5 Forbes Street,
Newtown, NSW 2042
Australia

For reasons of confidentiality, applications by telephone, fax or email will not be accepted.

MAKING A BEQUEST
TO THE TRUST

The Trust is endorsed as an Income Tax Exempt Charitable Entity under Subdivision 50-5 of the Income Tax Assessment Act 1997. The Trust is the holder of an authority under the provisions of Section 16 of the NSW Charitable Fundraising Act 1991. The ABN for the Trust is 99 069 920 550.

Anyone wishing to make a bequest to the Canon Jim Glennon Healing Ministry Trust may do so by direct deposit, with a cheque or money order sent to:

The Treasurer
The Canon Jim Glennon Healing Ministry Trust,
C/- The Healing Ministry Centre Golden Grove Ltd,
5 Forbes Street
Newtown, NSW 2042
Australia

Cheques or money orders should be crossed "Not Negotiable" and made payable to "The Canon Jim Glennon Healing Ministry Trust".

Alternatively, a bequest can be made from your Estate by instructing your solicitor to include a bequest notation in your "Last Will and Testament".